BASIC / NOT BORING
MATH SKILLS

GRAPHING, STATISTICS, & PROBABILITY

Grades 6–8⁺

Inventive Exercises to Sharpen
Skills and Raise Achievement

Series Concept & Development
by Imogene Forte & Marjorie Frank
Exercises by Marjorie Frank

Incentive Publications, Inc.
Nashville, Tennessee

About the cover:
Bound resist, or tie dye, is the most ancient known method of fabric surface design. The brilliance of the basic tie dye design on this cover reflects the possibilities that emerge from the mastery of basic skills.

Illustrated by Kathleen Bullock
Cover art by Mary Patricia Deprez, dba Tye Dye Mary®
Cover design by Marta Drayton and Joe Shibley
Edited by Angela L. Reiner

ISBN 0-86530-446-7

1   2   3   4   5   6   7   8   9   10   07   06   05   04
PRINTED IN THE UNITED STATES OF AMERICA
www.incentivepublications.com

TABLE OF CONTENTS

CELEBRATE BASIC MATH SKILLS

Basic does not mean boring! There certainly is nothing dull about . . .

 . . . calculating records for outrageous adventures such as egg-throwing, tightrope-walking, pancake-tossing, or sky surfing

 . . . graphing the upside-down spills of wild whitewater kayak racers or the flat tires of air-leaping freestyle bike tricksters

 . . . finding out about fast journeys on stilts, in taxis, on lawnmowers, or on unicycles

 . . . using statistics about shaving, haircutting, building, climbing, and other wild events

 . . . getting to know about accomplishments in bed-racing, bathtub-racing, wife carrying, and barefoot waterskiing

 . . . solving problems about snowboarding injuries and wakeboarding tricks, alligator-wrestling matches and marathon rollercoaster rides

 . . . figuring out the probability of catching a great surfing wave or winning a balloon race, or falling off a wild bull

These are just a few of the interesting adventures students can explore as they celebrate basic math skills with graphing, statistics, and probability. The idea of celebrating the basics is just what it sounds like . . . sharpening math skills while enjoying the wild excitement of extreme sports and wacky adventures. Each page of this book invites students to practice a high-interest math exercise sport. This is not just any ordinary fill-in-the-blanks way to learn. These exercises are fun and surprising, and they make good use of thinking skills. Students will do the useful work of practicing a specific graphing, statistics, or probability skill while stepping into a world of daredevil activities and wild fun.

The pages in this book can be used in many ways . . .

 • for individual students to sharpen a particular skill

 • with a small group needing to relearn or sharpen a skill

 • as an instructional tool for teaching a skill to any size group

 • by students working on their own

 • by students working under the direction of an adult.

Each page may be used to introduce a new skill, to reinforce a skill, or to assess a student's ability to perform a skill. You'll also find an appendix of resources helpful to students and teachers, including a ready-to-use test for assessing graphing, statistics, and probability skills.

As your students take on the challenges of these adventures with graphing, statistics, and probability, they will grow! And as you watch them check off the basic math skills they've strengthened, you can celebrate with them!

SKILLS CHECKLIST FOR GRAPHING, STATISTICS, & PROBABILITY

✔	SKILL	PAGE(S)
✓	Construct a frequency table from statistical data	10, 11
	Read & interpret tables of statistics	10-17, 28, 31, 32, 33, 34, 35
✓	Read & interpret frequency graphs (histograms)	12
✓	Construct a frequency graph from statistical data	13, 14
	Analyze data to find range and mean	16
	Analyze data to find median and mode	17
	Read & interpret a line graph	18, 21, 24, 36
	Read & interpret a bar graph	19, 22, 26, 27, 29, 30
✓	Construct a line graph from statistical data	20
	Read, interpret, & construct a circle graph	21
✓	Construct a bar graph from statistical data	22
✓	Read & interpret a multiple line graph	24
	Construct a multiple line graph from statistical data	25
	Read & interpret a double bar graph	26
	Construct a double bar graph	27
	Make interpretations & draw conclusions from data	28, 29
	Solve problems from statistics shown on a graph	30, 36
	Solve problems from statistical tables	31, 32, 33, 34, 35
	Describe possible outcomes of events	37-44, 47-49, 51, 52
	Identify events; find probability of an event	38-44, 47-52
	Describe all the possible outcomes of two events	40, 41, 42, 43
	Use tree diagrams to show possible outcomes of two actions	42, 43
	Use the counting principle to find possible outcomes	44
	Describe the permutations of sets	45
	Identify possible combinations of sets within a larger set	46
	Find the probability of independent events	47, 48
	Find the probability of dependent events	49
	Find the odds in favor or against the occurrence of an event	50
	Use probability concepts and calculations to solve problems	51
	Use random samplings to make probability predictions	52

GRAPHING,
STATISTICS,
&
PROBABILITY

Skills Exercises

ROLLER BLADE JUMP SCORES				
TRIXIE	7	4	0	2
DIXIE	6	5	7	6
KATE	10	9	9	7
MAY	6	7	2	9
JUMP:	1	2	3	4

GOING TO EXTREMES

Welcome to the Extreme Sports Event of the year!

Athletes are arriving to register for the competition. The box below shows data for the first 50 people in line to show which sport each one is here to enjoy. The data is in the form of letters, which are codes for different sports.

Finish the Frequency Table to show how many athletes in this group are registering for each of the sports.

EXTREME DATA

SPCL	SPCL	HGGD
AILS	AILS	BNGY
BNGY	HGGD	WSRF
WSRF	SPCL	BNGY
BCYS	WKBD	SKYS
HGGD	SKBD	AILS
SKBD	SKYS	JTSK
BFJP	WSRF	BNGY
JTSK	SPCL	AILS
WKBD	SKYS	SKYS
WKBD	JTSK	AILS
BFJP	HGGD	BNGY
SKBD	BNGY	JTSK
BNGY	WKBD	AILS
SKBD	WSRF	JTSK
JTSK	SKBD	BCYS
WKBD	JTSK	STLG

FREQUENCY TABLE
Sports Participation

SPORT	CODE	TALLY	FREQUENCY
jet skiers	JTSK		
windsurfers	WSRF		
aggressive in-line skaters	AILS		
barefoot waterski jumpers	BFJP		
bicycle stunt riders	BCYS		
skateboarders	SKBD		
street lugers	STLG		
hang gliders	HGGD		
skysurfers	SKYS		
wakeboarders	WKBD		
sport climbers	SPCL		
bungee jumpers	BNGJ		

Name

GOING TO EXTREMES, CONT.

The athletes at this year's competition come from all over the United States. The data shows the home state for each of the competitors. Use the data to complete the Frequency Table to show how many athletes live in each state represented.

FREQUENCY TABLE
Home States of Competitors

State	Tally	Number	State	Tally	Number
AK			MN		
AL			MO		
AR			MT		
AZ			NC		
CA			NJ		
CO			NM		
FL			NY		
GA			OR		
HI			SC		
ID			TX		
LA			WA		
ME			UT		
MI			VT		

EXTREME DATA

OR	WA	TX	AZ
ME	TX	UT	OR
CA	HI	CO	CO
MT	OR	HI	MT
ID	CA	ME	CO
CO	HI	CO	LA
CA	WA	CA	WA
HI	MT	CO	AK
GA	AL	AR	AL
WA	AK	HI	ID
CO	CA	ME	CO
HI	AK	HI	WA
ID	OR	NM	ME
MT	ID	HI	CA
CA	HI	MT	UT
SC	VT	NC	MI
MI	NY	SC	VT
HI	MT	UT	FL
CO	OR	HI	HI
WA	HI	CA	AK
AK	OR	AK	CO
CA	TX	WA	HI
CO	MT	CA	FL
FL	OR	HI	FL
NJ	CO	HI	CA
WA	CO	CA	NM
FL	HI	UT	MN
VT	ID	WA	CA
CA	AK	AK	AK
HI	HI	HI	CA
MO	CA	ID	CO
OR	CO	CA	MT

Name

WINTER EXTREMES

Competitors have been braving extreme weather conditions (blizzards, winds, and cold temperatures) to win medals in extreme winter sports. There is an extreme difference in the ages of the athletes this year.

Use the data on the histogram (frequency graph) to find out about their ages.

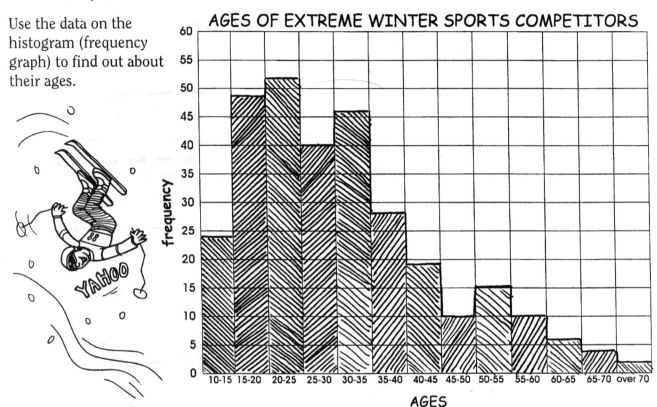

AGES OF EXTREME WINTER SPORTS COMPETITORS

1. Which age group has 19?_____

2. Which age group has 6?_____

3. Which age group has 28?_____

4. Which age group has 46 ? _____

5. Which age group has the most? _____

6. About 25 are in the _____ age group.

7. About 35 are _____or older.

8. About how many are 60 or older? _____

9. About how many are aged 10-20? _____

10. Which has about 20 less than the 30-35-year old group?_____

11. Which groups have less than the 45-50 year old group? _____

12. Which two groups have the same number?
_____

13. Which 10-year age span has about 30 competitors?_____

14. Which group has about the same as the 10-15 age group? _____

15. Which has about seven times as many competitors as the 60-65 year old group?
_____

16. Does the 35-40-year old age group have more than any younger groups? _____

Name _____

WINTER EXTREMES, CONT.

Some of the athletes have traveled long distances in the cold, winter weather to get to the Extreme Winter Competition. The Tally Sheet shows the travel frequencies.

Use this data to finish the frequency chart. For each mileage category on the graph, color a vertical bar to show the number of athletes traveling those distances.
Use a different color for each bar.

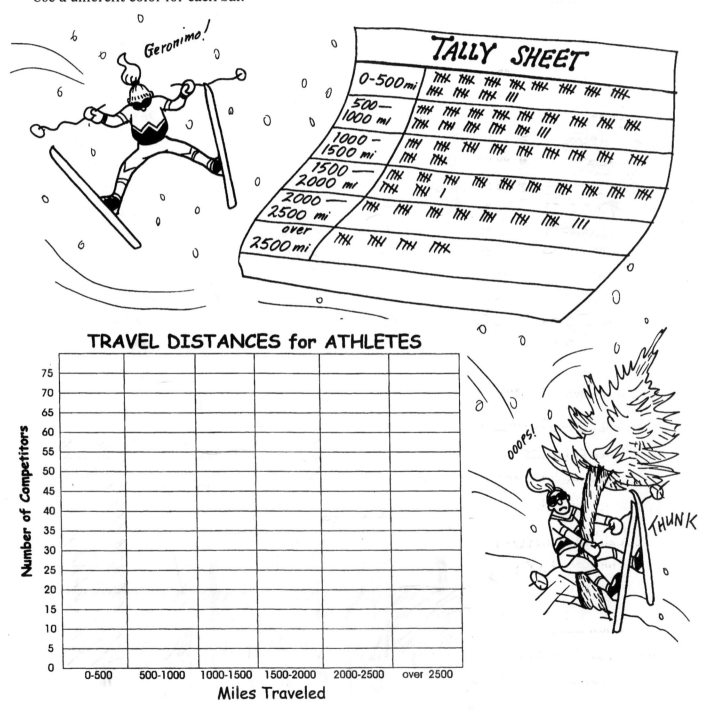

RECORD-SETTING ADVENTURES

It seems that people with a competitive spirit will go to any lengths to set (or break) a record! Here are some adventures where challengers set records for throwing, moving, jumping, driving, or spitting something the farthest.

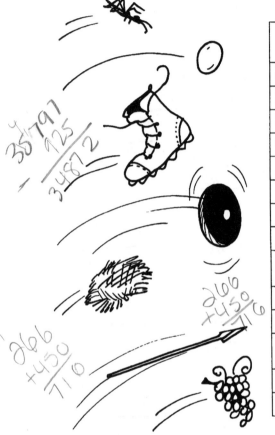

FAR-OUT ADVENTURES

Description of the Farthest.....	Record-Setting Distance
Egg Toss (without breaking the egg)	223 feet, 2 inches
Boot Throw	209 feet, 9 inches
Flying Disc Throw	656 feet, 2 inches
Cow Pie Throw	266 feet
Spear Throw	848 feet, 6 ½ inches
Grape Throw (caught in the mouth)	327 feet, 6 inches
Crawl	870 miles
Dance	23 miles, 385 yards
Cricket Spitting (Yes! People actually spit dead crickets in competition!)	32 feet, ½ inch
Ramp Jump in a Car	232 feet
Jump on a Motorcycle	251 feet
Underwater Dive (while holding breath)	925 feet
Underwater Dive (using equipment)	35,797 feet
Dive from a Diving Board	176 feet

1. Which went farther: the cow pie or the spear? _____

2. Which went farther: the egg or the grape? _____

3. Which went farther: the flying disc or the spear? _____

4. How much farther did the egg travel than the boot? _____

5. How much farther was the spear thrown than the boot? _____

6. How much farther did the motorcycle jump than the car? _____

7. How much farther did the crawler travel than the dancer? _____

8. Which went about 450 feet farther than the cow pie? _____

9. Which went about 75 feet farther than the diving board diver? _____

10. How much farther did the underwater diver with the equipment descend than the diver holding his breath did? _____

Name _____

AN EXTREMELY WET EVENT

Is it possible to complete a white-water rafting race without getting wet? These teams certainly took plenty of spills during the 5-day Wild Water Competition. The table shows the statistics for the number of tips and spills for each team. Use the tables to answer the questions below.

WHITE WATER RAFTING COMPETITION
UPSIDE-DOWN SPILLS

Team	# of Spills				
	Mon	Tue	Wed	Thur	Fri
Splashin' Six	20	19	5	0	3
White-Water Wizards	11	13	15	17	18
River Racers	7	1	1	0	2
Speed Demons	18	18	12	12	4
The Wet Ones	9	6	7	0	5
River Rats	5	9	2	6	1
The Untouchables	5	8	14	11	10
Floating Phantoms	5	15	19	19	7
The Rapids Racers	0	6	0	7	0
The Unsinkables	3	3	3	3	3
The Water Diggers	12	4	6	0	3
Kings of the Rapids	0	0	5	1	6

Find the total spills for:

1. The Splashin' Six _____

2. The White-Water Wizards _____

3. The River Racers _____

4. The Speed Demons _____

5. The Wet Ones_____

6. The River Rats _____

7. The Untouchables _____

8. The Floating Phantoms_____

9. The Rapids Racers _____

10. The Unsinkables_____

11. The Water Diggers _____

12. The Kings_____

13. Monday_____

14. Wednesday _____

15. Friday _____

16. Who had the most days with no spills? _____

17. Who had the fewest (total) spills?_____

18. Who had the most spills?_____

19. Which team had the same number each day? _____

20. Which day was the worst for spills?_____

21. Which day was the best for spills?(fewest spills)_____

22. Which team had more spills every day than the day before? _____

Name _____

FLIPS, TRICKS, & FLAT TIRES

In the BMX (bicycle motorcross) categories, nothing is quite as exciting as the freestyle and ramp riding competitions. Courageous bikers do wild tricks in the air: like spins, flips, rotations, wheelies, and hops. All that action can be hard on tires. Just look at how many went flat during this year's events!

Biker's Name	A.J. Ryder	J.R. Crash	Tom Elite	Gabe McTrick	Angie deWheel	B.J. Wynn	Z.Z. Tops	Flip Skyler
Number of Flat Tires	13	6	14	21	18	3	6	7

1. What is the range of the set of data? (Range is the difference between the least and greatest numbers.)

   _____

2. What is the mean of the set of data? (Mean is the sum of the data divided by the number of items.)

   _____

3. These are the numbers of quarts of water drunk by the different bikers: 7, 2, 4, 3, 5, 3, 6, 2.

   What is the range? _____

   What is the mean? _____

4. These are the weights of the bikers: 95 lb, 120 lb, 90 lb, 125 lb, 140 lb, 110 lb, 90 lb, 102 lb

   What is the range? _____

   What is the mean? _____

5. These are the numbers of falls the different bikers endured: 14, 5, 16, 14, 7, 1, 0, 9

   What is the range? _____

   What is the mean? _____

6. These are the numbers of injuries to the 8 different bikers: 16, 16, 22, 20, 15, 15, 32, 16

   What is the range? _____

   What is the mean? _____

Name

THE STRANGEST GAMES OF ALL

You might call this the Weird and Wacky Olympics! Competitors have gathered to join in contests and races of the strangest sort. The table gives data about the numbers of competitors in each event for five years of competitions.

Follow the directions to find the median (the middle number in a set of data) and the mode (the number that appears most frequently in a set of data) for the data given.

Numbers of Competitors, 1996-2000
The "Strange Games" Events

Sporting Event	1996	1997	1998	1999	2000
Sausage Eating	27	14	9	12	4
Alligator Wrestling	11	27	21	20	29
Bed Racing	18	30	18	20	32
Bathtub Racing	16	27	40	13	14
Ladder Climbing	15	33	6	20	10
Hair Cutting	21	16	21	20	9
Hand Sprinting	5	7	7	6	23
Pancake Tossing	11	15	21	2	9
Leapfrog Jumping	6	7	7	11	16
Egg Eating	10	9	15	15	9
Coconut Tree Climbing	11	4	21	20	11
Median					
Mode					

Finish the table by writing the median and mode for each year (each column).

Mush

1. Look at these scores from the egg-eating competition:

   14   26   12   22   15   18   9   20   6

   What is the median? _____

2. Look at these distances for the pancake toss:

   <u>54 ft</u>   <u>36 ft</u>   <u>52 ft</u>   <u>29 ft</u>   <u>50 ft</u>   <u>44 ft</u>   <u>56 ft</u>   <u>47 ft</u>   <u>39 ft</u>   <u>26 ft</u>   <u>36 ft</u>   <u>36 ft</u>

   What is the mode? _____

3. Look at these heights of coconut trees:

   7½ m   12 m   8½ m   10 m   14½ m   13m   17m

   What is the median? _____

4. Look at these weights of bathtubs used in the races:

   102 lb   98 lb   77 lb   101 lb   104 lb   77 lb   150 lb   116 lb   99 lb   115 lb   97 lb

   Circle the median. Draw a box around the mode.

Name _____

THE HUMAN SPIDER

Who, besides a spider, could possibly climb a building that is several hundred feet tall? Some pretty adventurous climbers try such ventures often!

Scaling buildings is another extreme idea for fun. Read the graph to find and learn about the heights of ten different buildings Spider Samson climbed last year.

1. Spider climbed the 348-meter T & C Tower in Taiwan in the month of _____ .

2. In July, he climbed the Shanghai World Finance Center, a height of _____ .

3. In _____ , he traveled to Thailand to climb the 319-meter Baiyoke II Tower.

4. South Africa's Carlton Center, which is _____ high, was an easy climb for Spider in March.

5. In the month of _____ , Spider reached the 381-meter top of the Empire State Building in New York City.

6. The Petronas Tower in Malaysia, climbed in June, is about _____ high.

7. Spider climbed the 347-meter John Hancock Center in Chicago in _____ .

8. In _____ and _____ , Spider climbed two Australian Towers: the 214-meter Chifley Tower and the 242-meter Rialto Tower.

9. In January and November, Spider climbed a church tower in his home town. It is _____ high.

Spider's Heights

Meters

500 —
400 —
300 —
200 —
100 —

Jan Feb Mar Apr May Jun Jly Aug Sep Oct Nov

Name _____

SURFING AT EXTREME HEIGHTS

Can you imagine riding a surfboard through the sky? What an idea! Skysurfers ride the wind, doing awesome tricks while they freefall from a plane. They can ride and fall for several thousand feet before opening a parachute. It may sound scary, but at least there are no sharks to worry about!

Nine different surfers jumped from a plane at 9500 feet. They each surfed while falling a distance through the air. The graph shows the number of vertical feet each one used for surfing before opening the parachute.

1. Sal's drop was about _____ feet.

2. Sly's drop was about _____ feet.

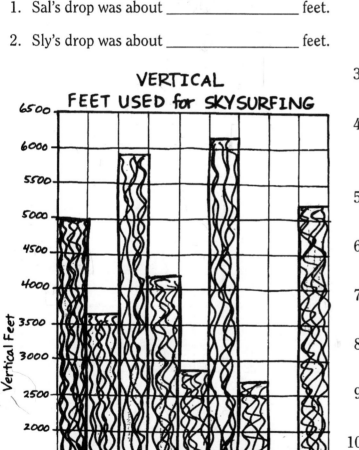

VERTICAL FEET USED for SKYSURFING

Vertical Feet

6500, 6000, 5500, 5000, 4500, 4000, 3500, 3000, 2500, 2000, 1500, 1000, 500

SID SAL SAM SUE SHER SLY SHIRL STU SARA

3. Who used more distance than Sara?
   _____

4. How many surfers used less distance than Sue?
   _____

5. Who surfed for 4250 feet?
   _____

6. Who used about 2700 feet to surf?
   _____

7. How many vertical feet did Sid use?
   _____

8. Who used about 5950 feet to surf?
   _____

9. How many less feet did Stu use than Sid? _____

10. Who used about 200 feet less than Sher? _____

11. Who surfed for a 5200-foot drop?
    _____

12. Whose drop was about 4500 feet greater than Stu's?
    _____

Name _____

SINKING TO EXTREME DEPTHS

Exploring shipwrecks is a favorite adventure for many scuba divers. Some of them will go to great depths to snoop around in ghostly, sunken ships.

The Data Table shows the depths of 12 different dives. Show the depths by completing the line graph. Finish labeling the intervals for feet measurements. Plot each data item. Then, draw the line to show the depths of the dives over a 12-day period.

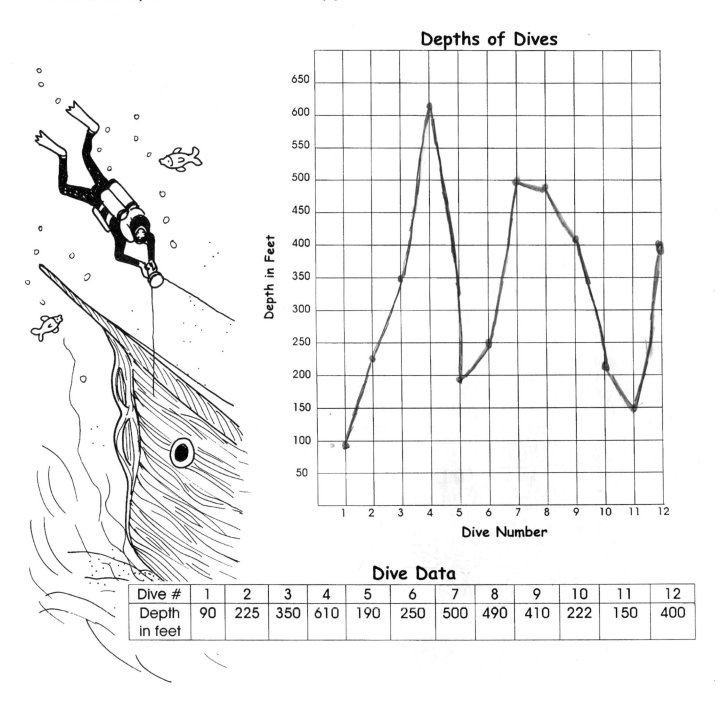

Depths of Dives

Dive Data

Dive #	1	2	3	4	5	6	7	8	9	10	11	12
Depth in feet	90	225	350	610	190	250	500	490	410	222	150	400

Name

SCUBA ECONOMICS

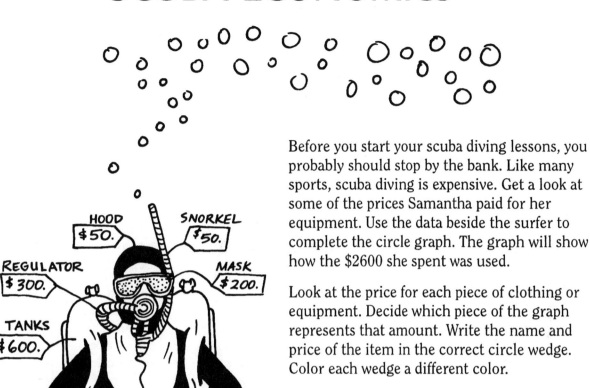

HOOD $50.

SNORKEL $50.

REGULATOR $300.

MASK $200.

TANKS $600.

GLOVES $50.

GAUGES $400.

KNIFE $100.

WET SUIT $800.

BOOTS $50.

FINS $100.

Before you start your scuba diving lessons, you probably should stop by the bank. Like many sports, scuba diving is expensive. Get a look at some of the prices Samantha paid for her equipment. Use the data beside the surfer to complete the circle graph. The graph will show how the $2600 she spent was used.

Look at the price for each piece of clothing or equipment. Decide which piece of the graph represents that amount. Write the name and price of the item in the correct circle wedge. Color each wedge a different color.

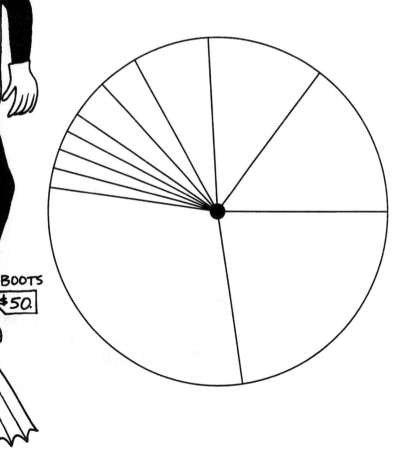

Name

BUMPS, BRUISES, OLLIES, & McTWISTS

Ollies, McTwists, fakies, iguana flips, tail grabs, back scratchers, nose roles, slob airs . . . these are some of the tricks snowboarders are doing as they sail up ramps and over jumps. Needless to say, they get a lot of injuries as they flip, turn, and crash!

The table shows data about the different injuries a team suffered during a recent season of competition. Use the data to finish the graph. Color a bar on the graph to show the correct number for each type of injury.

INJURIES

Kind of Injury	Number
Broken Legs	1
Broken Arms	2
Broken Feet	3
Broken Wrists or Fingers	6
Broken Noses	3
Broken Teeth	17
Sprained Ankles	5
Sprained Wrists or Fingers	28
Pulled Ligaments	23
Back Injuries	12
Head Injuries	5
Shoulder Injuries	25
Serious Cuts	32
Bloody Noses	26
Frostbite Cases	13
Serious Sunburn	22

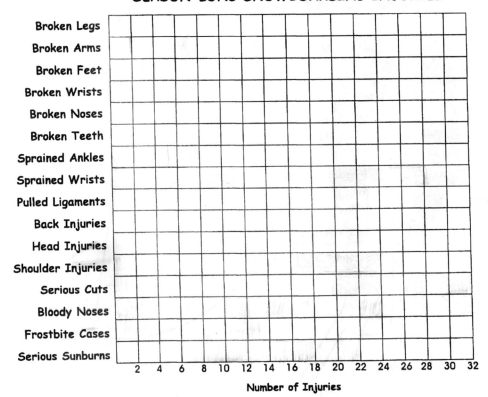

SEASON-LONG SNOWBOARDING INJURIES

Number of Injuries

Name

A SPORT WITH TEETH

Can this possibly be fun . . . wrestling a scaly reptile with snapping jaws and sharp teeth?
Some people must think it is, because they wrestle alligators for sport.

This scattergram gives some information about how often alligators bit the contestants at the Great
Gatorama Grappling Contest. Since a scattergram shows the relationship between two quantities,
you'll see that the number of bites is related to the size of each gator. Use the information from the
graph to answer the questions.

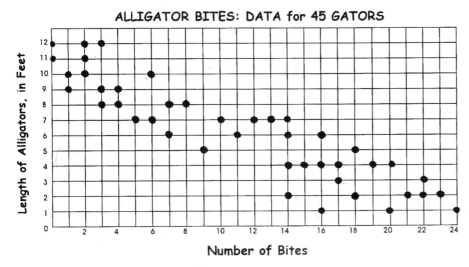

ALLIGATOR BITES: DATA for 45 GATORS

Length of Alligators, in Feet (y-axis)
Number of Bites (x-axis)

1. How many gators were 4 feet long? _____
2. How many gators were
   less than 4 feet long? _____
3. How many gators were 7 feet long? _____
4. How many gators were more than 8 feet long? _____
5. How long was the gator that bit 9 times?_____
6. How long was the gator that bit 24 times?_____
7. How long was the gator that bit 12 times?_____
8. Did a 3-foot gator bite less than 10 times?_____
9. Did a 6-foot gator bite 6 times? _____
10. Did a 10-foot gator bite more than 5 times? _____
11. What were the most times
    a 9-foot gator took a bite? _____
12. What lengths were the gators
    that did not bite at all? _____
13. What was the total number of bites
    from the 9-foot gators? _____
14. What was the least number of
    times a 2-foot gator took a bite? _____

15. Circle the statements which are
    true (according to the data):

    a. In general, the smaller gators
       bit more.

    b. In general, the larger alligators
       bit more.

    c. The length of the gator had no
       relationship to the number of
       bites.

    d. There were more gators 1–8
       feet long than 9–12 feet long.

    e. There were more 4-foot long
       gators than any other size.

    f. In general, the larger alligators
       bit less.

    g. The 11 and 12-foot long
       alligators did not bite at all.

Name _____

Basic Skills/Graphing, Statistics, & Probability 6-8+

NO WATER SKIS ALLOWED

No skis are needed at this waterskiing competition. The competitors ski and jump on their bare feet. The graph shows the jump scores for ten different jumps for each of four barefoot skiers. How well did they do?

1. Which skier had the most consistent scores?

   _____

2. Which skier had the greatest drop in score between 2 jumps in a row?

   _____

3. Which skier had the greatest rise in score between 2 jumps in a row?

   _____

4. Which skier probably won this competition? _____

5. Which skier scored below 12 most often?

   _____

6. Which skier made the best recovery from a drop in scores? _____

7. Do Nicole's 10 scores average above 14?

   _____

8. Did the majority of Brandy's scores fall above or below 12.0? _____

9. Between which 2 dives did Jennifer make the most improvement?

   _____

10. Between which 2 consecutive dives did Amanda make the most improvement?

    _____

11. Who had the third best score on the 9th dive?

    _____

12. Which skier received the score of 14.8 twice and 14.0 three times?

    _____

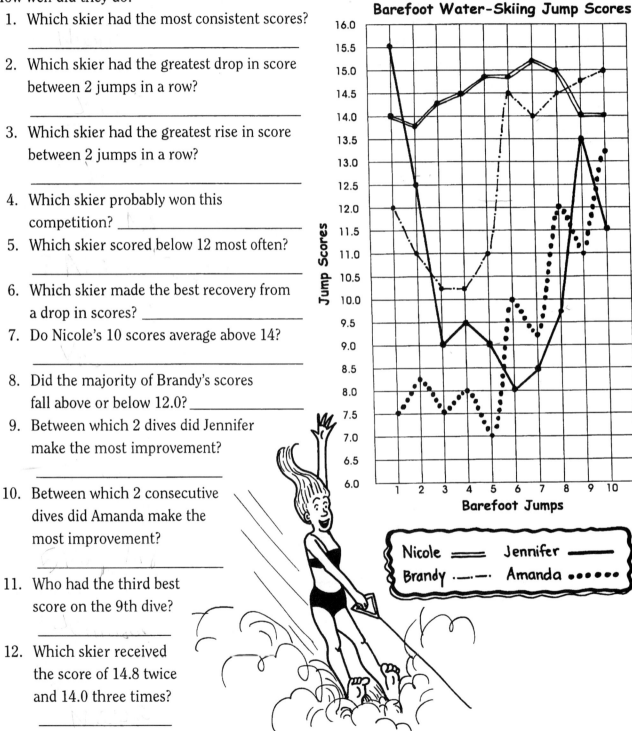

Barefoot Water-Skiing Jump Scores

Jump Scores / Barefoot Jumps

Nicole ═══ Jennifer ──────
Brandy ·─·─· Amanda ••••••

Name _____

EXTREME RISKS

Along with the thrill of most extreme sports comes a high risk factor. In all the sports, athletes use good equipment and follow rules to keep safe, but accidents are always a possibility. And when the sport takes place high up in the air above the ground, the accidents or injuries can be even more scary!

Three teams of friends from different sports kept track of the injuries each year over a 10-year period. The table shows the results of their count. Use this data to finish the line graph. Plot the amounts for each team for each year. Use the correct color of dots for each sport. Connect the dots with the line of the same color.

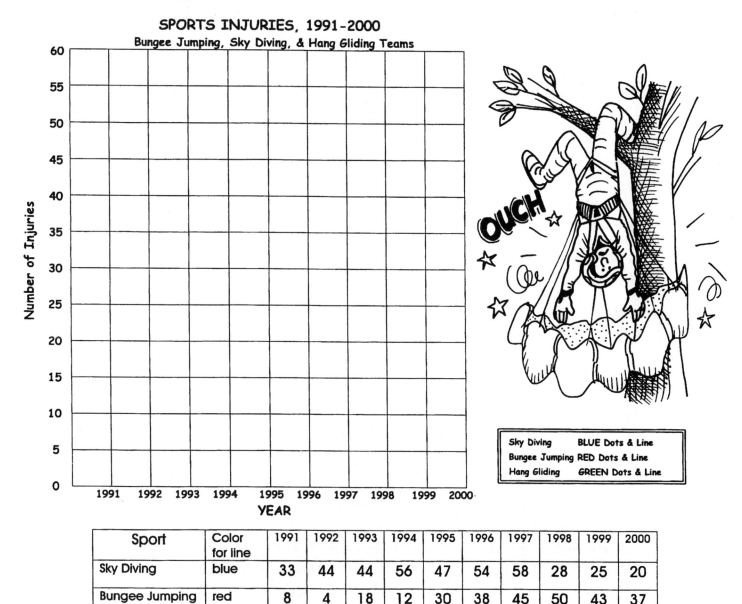

SPORTS INJURIES, 1991-2000
Bungee Jumping, Sky Diving, & Hang Gliding Teams

Sky Diving — BLUE Dots & Line
Bungee Jumping — RED Dots & Line
Hang Gliding — GREEN Dots & Line

Sport	Color for line	1991	1992	1993	1994	1995	1996	1997	1998	1999	2000
Sky Diving	blue	33	44	44	56	47	54	58	28	25	20
Bungee Jumping	red	8	4	18	12	30	38	45	50	43	37
Hang Gliding	green	20	26	19	38	55	59	60	56	60	60

Name

NO SLEEPING ALLOWED

Don't try to take a nap in any of these beds. They're being used for one of the world's most unusual sports . . . bed racing! Today's race is one mile long. The graph shows the record time for a 1-mile race for each team entering today. Also shown is each team's amount of experience at bed racing.

Use the data on the graph to answer the questions.

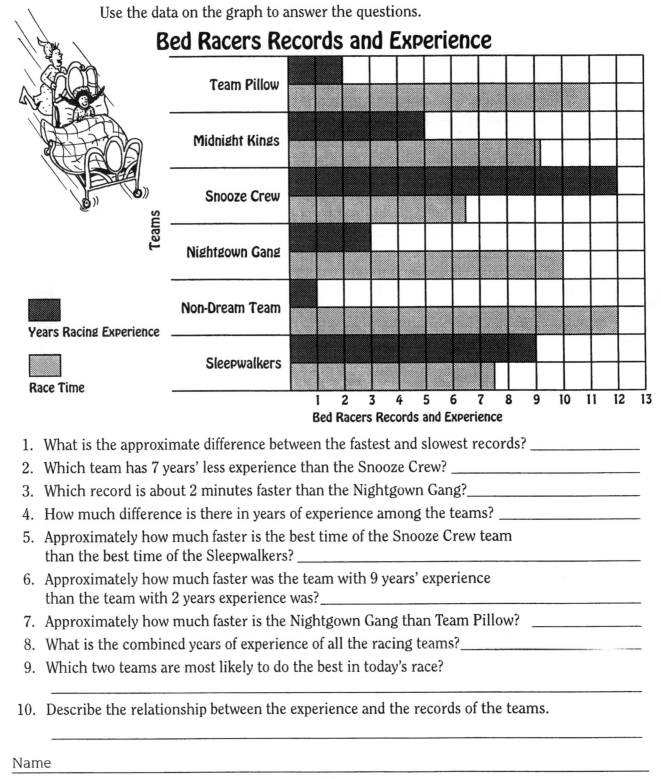

Bed Racers Records and Experience

1. What is the approximate difference between the fastest and slowest records? _____

2. Which team has 7 years' less experience than the Snooze Crew? _____

3. Which record is about 2 minutes faster than the Nightgown Gang? _____

4. How much difference is there in years of experience among the teams? _____

5. Approximately how much faster is the best time of the Snooze Crew team than the best time of the Sleepwalkers? _____

6. Approximately how much faster was the team with 9 years' experience than the team with 2 years experience was? _____

7. Approximately how much faster is the Nightgown Gang than Team Pillow? _____

8. What is the combined years of experience of all the racing teams? _____

9. Which two teams are most likely to do the best in today's race?

_____

10. Describe the relationship between the experience and the records of the teams.

_____

Name _____

ICY CLIMBING

You can find adventuresome people climbing frozen surfaces all over the world. The ice-climbing competition is a "hot" event at the Extreme Winter Games, too.

An ice climber can win medals for climbing speed or for difficulty. The table below shows some data for five ice-climbing friends. Use the data on the table to finish the graph. For each climber, color a green bar (on the left) to show the number of medals won for climbing speed, and a yellow bar (on the right) to show the number of medals won for climbing difficulty.

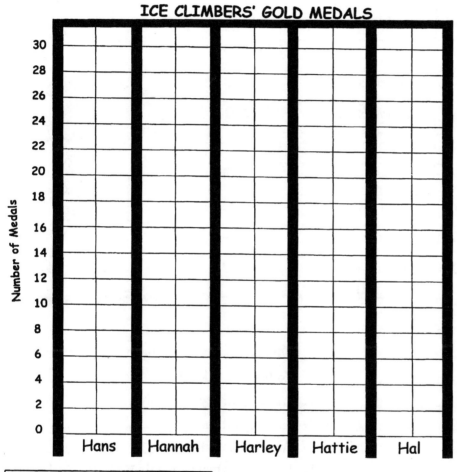

ICE CLIMBERS' GOLD MEDALS

Number of Medals — 0, 2, 4, 6, 8, 10, 12, 14, 16, 18, 20, 22, 24, 26, 28, 30

Hans   Hannah   Harley   Hattie   Hal

Use GREEN to show medals for speed
Use YELLOW to show medals for difficulty

Climber	# of Gold Medals Won for Speed	# of Gold Medals Won for Difficulty
Hans	19	16
Hannah	10	20
Harley	29	6
Hattie	23	24
Hal	13	27

Name

EXTREME JOURNEYS

A journey can be taken in many ways . . . on foot, by sled, on stilts, on hands and knees, in a wheelchair, on skates . . . or even just walking on hands. Here are statistics about some records set for the most unusual journeys. These distances are almost unbelievable! Use the data to answer the questions.

RECORDS for EXTREME JOURNEYS

(According to 1999 Guinness Book of World Records, Rounded to the nearest mile)

Journey	Distance in Miles	Journey	Distance in Miles
Taxi	21,691	Polar Sled	3,750
Motorcycle	457,000	Bicycle	226,800
Snowmobile	10,252	Backwards Walk	8,000
Lawn Mower	3,366	Backwards Run	3,100
Wheelchair	24,903	Hitchhike	501,750
Unicycle	2,361	Stilt Walk	3,008
Walk on Hands	870	Walk on Water	3,502
Leapfrog	996	Parachute Fall	6
Skates	19,000	Unicycle, riding backwards	53
Crawling	870	Dancing	23

1. How much farther did the motorcycle travel than the bicycle? _____

2. Which record is the longest distance for a journey that did not involve a motorized vehicle? _____

3. How much further did the backwards walker travel than the backwards runner? _____

4. How much shorter was the dancer's journey than the crawler's? _____

5. Which record surprises you most? _____

   Why? _____

6. Which appears to be more difficult: a journey on skates, or walking on your hands? _____

7. Which journey probably took the longest time? _____

   Why do you think so? _____

8. Which journey probably took the least time? _____

   Why do you think so? _____

9. What is the difference between the record times for the frontwards and backwards unicycle rides? _____

10. From what the data tells you, does it appear to be easier to travel while crawling or dancing? _____

Name _____

RIDING THE WAKE

Stay awake when you're riding the wake! An exciting new sport, called wakeboarding takes advantage of the thrill of riding the crest of water created behind a motor boat. Wakeboarders use the power of the wake to do all kinds of fancy tricks.

Walter is practicing his wakeboarding tricks. He wants to do 30 of each in good form this week. How is he doing so far? Use the information on the graph to answer the questions.

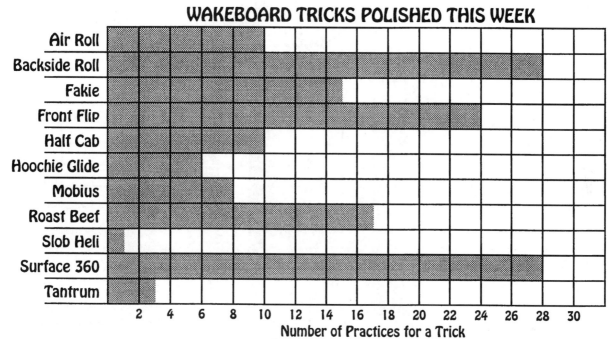

WAKEBOARD TRICKS POLISHED THIS WEEK

Number of Practices for a Trick

1. How many good front flips does Walter have left to do this week to reach his goal? _____
2. How many more good roast beefs does Walter need? _____
3. How many more half cabs has he done than hoochie glides? _____
4. How many more backside rolls has he done than air rolls? _____
5. How many more good tantrums is he working for this week? _____
6. How many more front flips has he done than roast beefs? _____
7. Does Walter seem to be doing well at polishing his surface 360s? _____
8. How many more times does he need a good practice of a mobius to meet his goal? _____
9. Which appears to be harder for Walter, the fakie or the half cab?_____

Yahoo!

10. Which trick seems to be giving Walter the most trouble in his work to complete 30 good samples of each? _____
11. Today is Tuesday (night). If he continues accomplishing his goals at the same rate as he has since Sunday, will Walter have all his 30 good roast beefs by Saturday night? _____
12. Will he have 30 good half cabs by Saturday night, continuing at this pace? _____

Name _____

EXTREME THRILLS

Bungee Jumping is perhaps the wildest thrill of all the sports! Brave people of all ages leap off high places, attached only by a stretchy, bouncy cord that lets them fall, then bounces them back and forth for a while. More and more adventuresome folks are trying group bungee jumping . . . leaping while grouped together with many other jumpers.

The graph shows data which compares ages of some bungee jumpers to the number of jumps they've taken in the past year. Use the data to solve the problems.

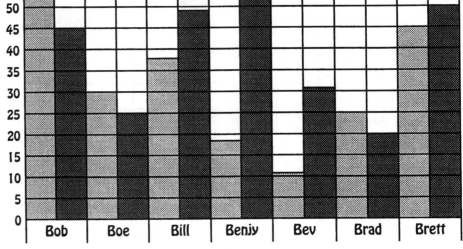

BUNGEE JUMPERS: JUMPS & AGES

1. What is the difference in age between the oldest and youngest jumpers?

   _____

2. What is the difference between the greatest and least number of jumps? _____

3. For which jumpers is this statement true?
   A (age of jumper) > N (number of jumps)

   _____

   _____

4. Is this statement true? **The youngest 2 jumpers together did more jumps than the oldest 2 jumpers.** _____

5. The 56-year old did how many more jumps than the 25-year old? _____

6. The 11-year old did how many more jumps than the 25-year old? _____

7. In the following statement, who is x and who is y *(x and y stand for the number of jumps)*?
   x − y = 19
   x =   y =

8. In the following statement, who is x and who is y *(x and y stand for the number of jumps)*?
   3y = x
   x =   y =

9. In the following statement, who is a and who is b *(a and b stand for the ages)*?
   b ≐ 2 a + 6
   a =   b =

10. What is the average age of the jumpers *(round to nearest whole number)*? _____

Name _____

EXTREMELY HIGH WALKING

It is a very long way down from the place where this extreme activity takes place. Tightrope walkers spend years practicing their art high above the ground. Some walkers go to great heights without any sort of safety net at all.

The table shows the records for a group of tightrope walking friends. Notice that the record height and the record length (distance) is included for each of twelve tightrope walkers.

Use the data to solve the problems below.

Records for Tightrope Walks
Mile High County Tightrope Club

Tightrope Walker	Record Height of Wire (in feet)	Record Length of Walk (in feet)
Francine	430	48
Flossie	610	45
Frankie	225	30
Frenchie	80	55
Phillipe	610	35
Flo	390	72
Phyllis	850	29
Flip	1000	120
Fran	305	85
Phoebe	700	29
Frank	903	68
Fred	275	72

1. How much higher has Frank performed than Frankie?_____

2. How much longer a distance did Flo walk than Flossie? _____

3. Who walked about twice the distance as Phillipe? _____

4. Who walked about one-fourth the distance as Flip?_____

5. Whose record height was twice as high as Fran's? _____

6. Who performed at a height 513 feet higher than Flo? _____

7. Who has performed almost twice as high as Francine? _____

8. What is the difference between Phillipe's record for height and Flossie's? _____

9. How much higher has Fred performed than Frenchie?_____

10. Who performed at a height 150 feet higher than Phoebe?_____

11. How many club members have performed at greater heights than Francine? _____

12. How much difference is there between the longest
    and the shortest of the records for length of walk? _____

13. How much difference is there between the greatest
    and the least records for height of wire?_____

14. If a new performer successfully walks 81 feet across a wire,
    how many records of other club members will this exceed? _____

Name _____

LONG HOURS & STEEP DROPS

The highest rollercoaster in the United States is Superman, The Escape, at Six Flags Magic Mountain in California. There is a 415 foot distance between its base and its highest peak.

Marco and several friends have caught "rollercoaster fever." They love the thrill of those steep drops—over and over. They compete with each other for rollercoaster-riding records, riding different coasters for as long as they can at one time. (They stop to sleep occasionally.) The table shows the lengths of times different riders spent on different coasters. Use the data to solve the problems on the next page.

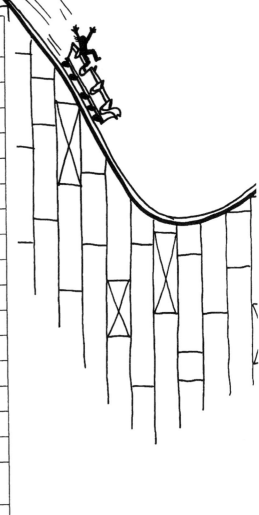

ROLLERCOASTER RIDES

Name of Coaster	Location of Rollercoaster	Length of Ride (Hours)
Silver Bullet	Oklahoma City, OK	18
The Cannonball	Gulf Shores, AL	73
Shockwave	Gurnee, IL	29
Twisted Sisters	Louisville, KY	52
Red Devil	Maggie Valley, NC	23
Big Bad Wolf	Williamsburg, VA	44
Desert Storm	Phoenix, AZ	66
Desperado	Primm, NV	50
Batman, The Ride	Atlanta, GA	20
Black Widow	Agawam, MA	110
Top Gun	Santa Clara, CA	83
Steel Phantom	West Mifflin, PA	55
Mean Streak	Sandusky, OH	70
Swamp Fox	Myrtle Beach, SC	31
Tidal Wave	Ocean City, MD	52
Colossal Fire Dragon	Farmington, UT	93
Great American Scream Machine	Jackson, NJ	88
The Outlaw	Des Moines, IA	39
Texas Twister	Houston, TX	52
Mind Eraser	Denver, CO	7

Name

LONG HOURS & STEEP DROPS, CONT.

1. Marco rode in Arizona and Alabama. What was his total time on these rides? _____

2. Mei Chen rode one coaster for 110 hours. In what state did she ride? _____

3. How much longer was Marco's ride on Top Gun than on Big Bad Wolf? _____

4. Joe rode in Utah and Georgia last week. How long did he ride? _____

5. How much longer was the longest ride than the shortest ride? _____

6. How many hours were ridden all together by Marco and his friends? _____

7. Marco's favorite ride was for 83 hours. What state was this in?_____

8. Which ride was twice as long as the ride on the Steel Phantom? _____

9. Which ride was about 1/3 as long as the ride on the Colossal Fire Dragon?_____

10. How much shorter was the Outlaw ride than the Steel Phantom ride? _____

11. Pete rode these three coasters in one week: Mind Eraser, Swamp Fox, and Shockwave.
    How long did he ride that week? _____

12. Angelo rode Silver Bullet and Desperado. Maria rode the Mean Streak.
    Whose riding time was longer? _____
    How much longer?_____

13. Which coaster was ridden half as long as the ride on Great American Scream Machine?
    _____

14. Brianna rode in Kentucky, Pennsylvania, and Maryland.
    Pete rode in South Carolina, Illinois, and Texas. Who rode longer? _____

15. Which three coasters were ridden the same amount of time? _____

    What was the total of the hours ridden on these three?_____

16. Which coaster was ridden 16 hours longer than the Red Devil? _____

Name _____

EXTREME ACHIEVEMENTS

Could you make a bed in 28 seconds, or eat 6 pounds of sausage in 3 minutes, or give a haircut in 2 minutes? It's amazing what people can do when they are motivated to set records! The table on the next page gives some intriguing data about the extreme achievements people can accomplish when they catch the competitive spirit.

Use the table to solve the problems on the next page.

ACHIEVEMENTS IN RECORD TIME
(According to the 1999 Guinness Book of World Records)

Achievement **The fastest...**	Details	Record Time
Hot dog eater	ate 30 hot dogs	64 sec
Pancake tosser	tossed 416 pancakes, one at a time	2 min
Hand sprinter	sprinted 164 feet on hands	16.93 sec
Yodeler	yodeled 27 tones	1 sec
Drummer	played 400 different drums	16.2 sec
Banana eater	ate 17 peeled bananas	2 min
Coconut tree climber	climbed 9-meter tree	4.88 sec
Haircutter	gave 1 haircut	2 min, 20 sec
Shaver	shaved 1 face	12.9 sec
Bed Racer	raced a bed 2 miles, 56 yards	12 min, 9 sec
Wife carrier	carried wife 771 feet	1 min, 5 sec
Talker	spoke 595 words	56.01 sec
Egg eater	ate 13 raw eggs	1 sec
Bed maker	made 1 bed	28.2 sec
Bathtub racer	raced a bathtub 36 miles	1 hr, 22 min, 27 sec
Shoe shiner	4-member team shined 14,975 shoes	8 hr
Lemon eater	ate 3 whole lemons, (peels & seeds too)	15.3 sec
Spaghetti eater	ate 100 yards of spaghetti	12.02 sec

Name _____

EXTREME ACHIEVEMENTS, CONT.

Use the table on page 34 to solve the problems.

1. How far did the tree climber climb per second? _____

2. About how much distance did the hand sprinter travel per second? *(Circle one.)*
       1.6 ft   16.4 ft   10 ft   100 ft   0.16 ft

3. About how many shoes did the shoe shiners finish in an hour? _____

4. Did the talker speak about 1 word per 0.01 second? _____

5. Did the bathtub racers travel at a speed of more than 40 mph? _____

6. How long did it take for the spaghetti eater to eat each yard? _____

7. How many pancakes did the pancake tosser toss per minute? _____

8. About how much time did the drummer spend drumming each drum? _____

9. How much shorter was the drumming than the handsprint? _____

10. How long did it take for the hot dog eater to eat one dog? _____

Assuming the event could go on at the same rate shown . . . .

11. How many tones could the yodeler yodel in a minute? _____

12. Could the bed racer cover 8 miles in an hour? _____

13. About how many people could the shaver shave in one hour? *(Circle one.)*
        20   50   500   300   100

14. Could the haircutter give 30 haircuts in one hour? _____

15. How many raw eggs could the egg eater swallow in a minute? _____

16. How long would it take to get a haircut and a shave? _____

17. About how long would it take to carry the wife a mile? *(Circle one.)*
        70 min   17 min   7½ min   30 min

18. About how long would it take the bed makers to make 6 beds? *(Circle one.)*
        3 min   2 min   5 sec   15 min   1.5 min

Name _____

LONG-JUMPING MOTORCYCLES

In 1997, Fiona Beale, of Derby, England, jumped 190 feet, 2 inches over 12 trucks. She was riding a Kawasaki KX500 when she became the new record-holder for the longest distance jumped by a woman on a motorcycle.

Motorcycle jumping is a thrill for the rider, and a thrill for spectators, too. Four thrill-seeking competitors (B. J., J. J., R. J., and P. J.) showed their expertise by challenging each other to a week-long jumping contest. The graph shows the number of cars each challenger jumped every day for five days. Use the graph to solve the problems.

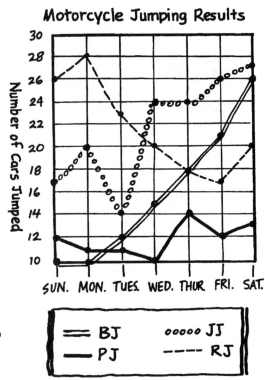

Motorcycle Jumping Results

1. What is the total of all R. J.'s jumps? _____
2. Whose average of all 7 jumps was less than 12? _____
3. What is the average of all the jumps on Monday? _____
4. Is R. J.'s average jump for the week more than 15 cars? _____
5. Which jumpers have the same total number of jumps? _____ _____ _____
6. What is the difference between J. J.'s best and worst jumps? _____
7. Whose best jump is almost twice her own worst jump? _____

8. Whose worst jump cleared more cars than P. J.'s best jump? _____
9. On Wednesday, who jumped 50% of the cars as R. J.? _____
10. On Thursday, who jumped 75% of the cars that J. J. jumped? _____
11. Who had the greatest difference between her best and worst jumps? _____
12. Who jumped twice the cars on Monday that J. J. jumped on Tuesday? _____
13. The expression **x – 14** can be used to represent the number of cars P. J. jumped on Saturday. Whose jump is represented by **x**? _____
14. At the last competition, P. J. jumped 100 cars. How many more is that than this week's total? _____

Name _____

TO RIDE A WILD BULL

Sometimes they stay on. Sometimes they fall off! Riders of wild bulls have plenty of experience with falls, throws, and flying trips through the air.

Staying on the bull may be a matter of skill. Today, since all the riders are brand new, it's a matter of chance.

The probability of an event that is impossible is 0. The probability of an event that is certain is 1.

When you don't know the outcome, the probability is somewhere between 0 and 1, usually expressed as a fraction; staying on the bull is somewhere between 0 and 1.

> For each bull rider in today's contest, there are four possible results or outcomes that may occur. Assume there is an equal probability of all four shown on the chart.
> 1. The probability of F1 (falling off before the 1st bell) = P (F1) = ¼
> 2. P (F2) = _____
> 3. P (not falling at all) = P (S1 + S2) = _____
> 4. P (falling) = P (F1 + F2) = _____

POSSIBLE OUTCOMES FOR BULL RIDERS	
F1	Fall off before 1st bell
S1	Stay on just until 1st bell
F2	Fall off between 1st & 2nd bells
S2	Stay on until 2nd bell

Write a number to show the probability for each of these. It will be 0, 1, or a fraction between 0 and 1.

5. The sun will rise tomorrow. _1_

6. A coin toss will yield heads. _.5_

7. 2 odd numbers will have an even sum. _.5_

8. The sun will set in the east. _0_

9. You'll spend the summer on the moon. _0_

10. If you toss one die, you will get a 6. _.15_

11. 2 even numbers will have an even sum. _1_

12. You will have homework today. _.5_

13. The next president of the United States will be from your state. _.02_

14. Winter will follow fall. _1_

What are the number of possible outcomes for these events?

15. Flip of a coin _2_

16. Toss of one die _6_

17. Choosing a month beginning with J _3_

18. Choosing a day beginning with T _2_

19. How many possible outcomes are there from spinning this spinner? _5_

20. Which is the most likely? _E_

21. Which is the least likely? _C_

22. Which outcomes are equally likely? _A & B_

Name

EXTREMELY AWESOME BIKE TRICKS

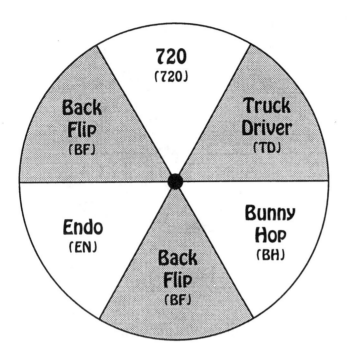

Freestyle bike tricks are exciting events to watch. The adventuresome bikers do wild tricks like Bunny Hops (hopping the bike into the air), Back Flips (jumping in the air and spinning around once, then "sticking" the landing), 720s (performing two full 360° rotations in the air), Truck Drivers (spinning the handlebar while doing a 360° rotation in the air), and Endos (balancing on the front wheel of the bike).

The bikers will start the competition with a spin of the spinner to tell them which trick to try. The set of one or more outcomes from the spinner is called an event. Tell the probability of the events described below.

Remember: P(E event) = $\dfrac{\text{number of a particular outcome}}{\text{number of possible outcomes}}$

1. P(EN) = _____

2. P(BF) = _____

3. P(TD) = _____

4. P(BF or TD) = _____

5. P(anything but BF) = _____

6. P(BH or 720) = _____

7. P(720) = _____

8. P (EN or BF) = _____

Use the numbered spinner to find the probability of these events:

9. P(odd number) = _____

10. P(prime number) = _____

11. P(10 or 15) = _____

12. P(less than 14) = _____

13. P(divisible by 3) = _____

14. P(multiple of 2) = _____

15. P(sum of digits < 3) = _____

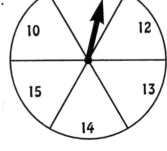

16. P(greater than 10) = _____

17. P(sum of digits is 6) = _____

18. P(multiple of 5) = _____

Name _____

EQUALLY AWESOME SKI TRICKS

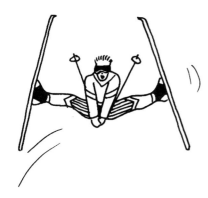

Freestyle skiing is even more thrilling to perform than it is to watch (although the watching is definitely easier and safer). Three kinds of tricks fit into the freestyle category. Skiers may do all three, but they often excel in one. Aerial tricks involve fancy jumps in the air. Acro tricks are airborne ballet moves. In mogul skiing, athletes ski over bumps, often doing tricks as they bounce up into the air.

The chart shows the numbers of skiers from three countries specializing in each of the three kinds of tricks. Finish the chart. Then find the probability of each event.

Country		AR (Aerials)	AC (Acro)	M (Moguls)	Totals for each Country
J	Japan	20	10	20	_____
C	Canada	10	50	30	_____
U	USA	20	20	20	_____
	Totals	_____	_____	_____	_____

You meet a skier. What is the probability . . . .

1. P(Skier is from C) = _____

2. P(Skier is not from U) = _____

3. P(Skier is from J) = _____

4. P(Skier is a mogul skier from C) = _____

5. P(Skier is an aerial skier from J) = _____

6. P(Skier is not an acro skier) = _____

7. P(Skier is mogul or acro skier) = _____

8. P(Skier is not a mogul skier) = _____

9. P(Skier is an aerial skier from U) = _____

10. P(Skier is an acro skier from C) = _____

11. You meet a USA skier.
    P(Skier is an M skier) = _____

12. You meet a Japanese skier.
    P(Skier is not an AC skier) = _____

13. You meet a Canadian skier.
    P(Skier does not ski M) = _____

14. You meet an acro skier.
    P(Skier is from J) = _____

15. You meet an aerial skier.
    P(Skier is from J or U) = _____

16. You meet a USA skier.
    P(Skier is AR or AC) = _____

17. You meet a mogul skier.
    P(Skier is from C) = _____

18. You meet an aerial skier.
    P(Skier is not from U) = _____

19. You meet an acro skier.
    P(Skier is from C) = _____

20. You meet a Japanese skier.
    P(Skier is an AC skier) = _____

Name _____

TAKING CHANCES ON THE RIVER

Kayaking is a wild sport, with plenty of wild white water, thrills, and spills.

These kayakers spin to choose which one of the three runs they will take down the river. The race takes two days. Each kayaker spins each day.

What are the possible outcomes for two spins? List them on the chart. Use the letter codes.

OUTCOMES for 2 Spins		

Use the chart to find the probabilities:

1. P(D one of the days) = _____

2. P(R neither day) = _____

3. P(N both days) = _____

4. P(R and D on the 2 days) = _____

5. P(same run both days) = _____

6. P(different runs both days) = _____

Kayak Runs

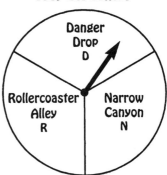

After the routes are chosen, each pair of racers flips a coin to see who does the run first. Alexander always calls for heads. See how he did at starting first in four different races. Use the chart to list all the possible outcomes for flipping a coin four times.

7. P(Alexander started first) = _____

8. P(two of each) = _____

9. P(three of one) = _____

10. P(4 heads or 4 tails) = _____

11. P(no heads) = _____

12. P(HTTH or THHT) = _____

OUTCOMES FOR 4 FLIPS			

Name

TAKING CHANCES ON THE RIVER, CONT.

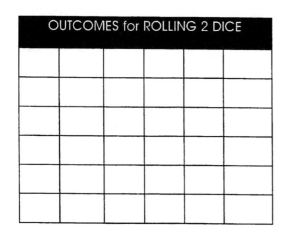

OUTCOMES for ROLLING 2 DICE

Sometimes the kayakers use dice to decide who will go first in the race. Each athlete rolls the dice, and they watch for the highest sum of the two dice.

Finish the table to show all the possible outcome when two dice are rolled. Write the outcomes this way (first roll, second roll) e.g., (4,6).

Find the probabilities:

1. P(6,6) = _____

2. P(both numbers the same) = _____

3. P(2 even numbers) = _____

4. P(2 prime numbers) = _____

5. P(2 odd numbers) = _____

6. P(sum of 6) = _____

7. P(sum of > 10) = _____

8. P(sum of 8) = _____

9. P(sum an even number) = _____

10. P(sum of 10) = _____

11. P(sum of < 5) = _____

12. P(sum of 9) = _____

13. P(difference of 4) = _____

14. P(difference of 1) = _____

15. P(difference of 5) = _____

16. P(sum of 11) = _____

Name _____

FOLLOWING THE WIND

You don't need an ocean for this kind of surfing. But you do need wind. Windsurfers travel to the places where they can usually count on high winds to sweep them along rivers and other bodies of water on a surfboard attached to a sail.

Of course, they hope for excellent winds every day. Sometimes the winds are less than top speed, but are okay for good surfing. Other days, the winds are just downright poor for the sport. On two consecutive days of judging the winds, what are the possible outcomes? A tree diagram can be used to show the number of outcomes. Finish the tree diagram to show all the possible outcomes on the diagram.

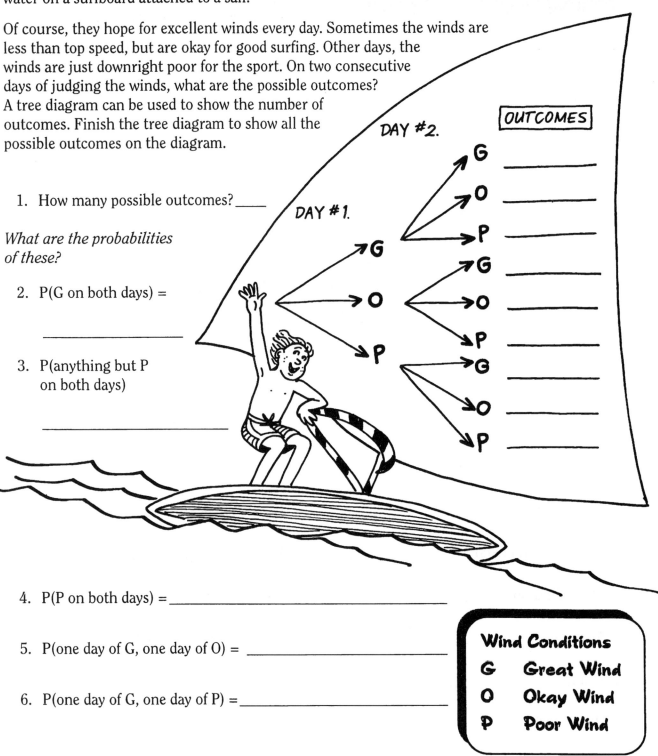

1. How many possible outcomes? ____

What are the probabilities of these?

2. P(G on both days) =

   _____

3. P(anything but P on both days)

   _____

4. P(P on both days) = _____

5. P(one day of G, one day of O) = _____

6. P(one day of G, one day of P) = _____

Wind Conditions

G   Great Wind

O   Okay Wind

P   Poor Wind

FOLLOWING THE WIND, CONT.

Today there is prize money waiting for the top finishers in the windsurfing races.
There are two races, and two chances to win. With five racers, each racer has a chance to come in
1st, 2nd, 3rd, 4th, or 5th.

PRIZES

1st	$200
2nd	$100
3rd	$ 80
4th	$ 50
5th	$ 0

1st both days $500

What are the possibilities for Miranda's finishes in two races?
Use the tree diagram to show all the possible outcomes for her.

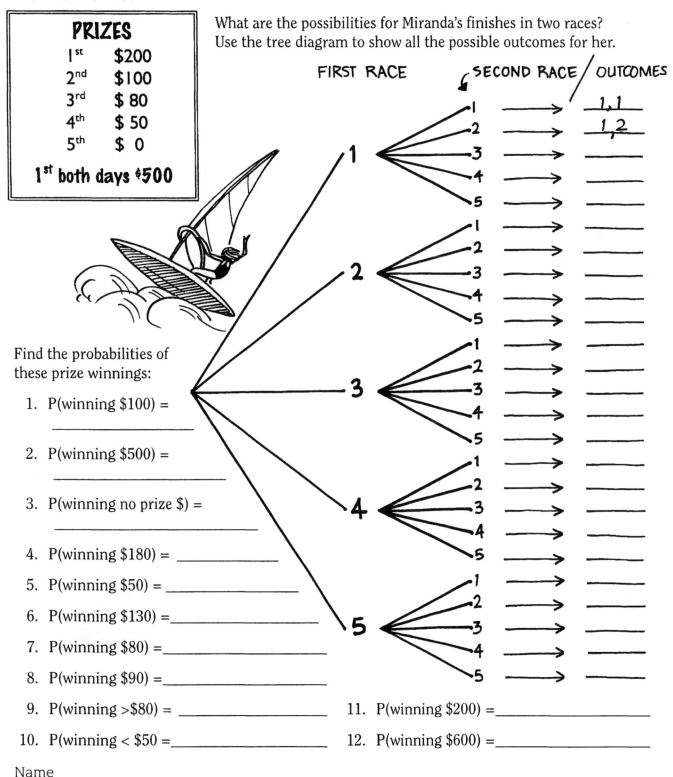

FIRST RACE   SECOND RACE / OUTCOMES

Find the probabilities of
these prize winnings:

1. P(winning $100) = _____

2. P(winning $500) = _____

3. P(winning no prize $) = _____

4. P(winning $180) = _____

5. P(winning $50) = _____

6. P(winning $130) =_____

7. P(winning $80) =_____

8. P(winning $90) =_____

9. P(winning >$80) = _____

10. P(winning < $50 =_____

11. P(winning $200) =_____

12. P(winning $600) =_____

Name

FAST TRACKS

Making tracks through the snow is the hobby for snowmobilers . . . and the faster the tracks are, the better.

In this snowmobile race, there is more than one way to make tracks from Start to Finish. Sometimes counting is the most practical way to find the number of outcomes for a probability problem. This is one of those times. Find out the number of possible outcomes by counting the snowmobile routes.

START

FROZEN FAST TRACK

SLIPPERY SLOPE

WIND WHIP WAY

RIDGE RIDER

HIP-HOP DROP

SNOWSHOE HILL

NECK BREAKER POINT

AVALANCHE ALLEY

ICE-CREAM SLOPE

SERPENTINE TRAIL

FINISH

1. Number of routes from START to Snowshoe Hill _____

2. Number of routes from Snowshoe Hill to Neckbreaker Point _____

3. Number of routes from Neckbreaker Point to the FINISH line _____

4. Routes from START to FINISH = # from START to SH x # NP x # to FINISH

   = _____ x _____ x _____ = _____

   (If you want to, try listing all the routes on another piece of paper.)

5. What is the probability Chuck took this route in the race: Slippery Slope to Snowshoe Hill, Wind Whip Way to Neckbreaker Point, and Ice Cream Slope to the FINISH? _____

6. What is the number of possible routes from A to D? _____

7. What is the number of possible routes from 1 to 5? _____

8. What is the number of possible routes from W to Z? _____

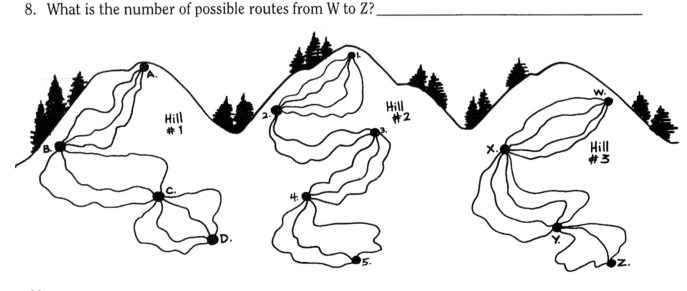

HIGH ALTITUDE RACING

Hot air balloons of all sizes, shapes, and designs are scattered through the sky during a balloon race. The imaginations of the balloon designers seem to be unlimited. In this race, these three balloons (the mouse, the cat, the piece of cheese) are the first ones to approach the finish line.

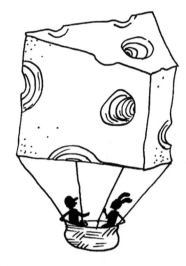

There are several different ways they could finish in 1st, 2nd, and 3rd place. The different arrangements, or orders, in which they could finish, are called **permutations**.

Finish the chart to write down all the possible arrangements.

How many permutations? _____

PERMUTATIONS for 3 BALLOONS		
CH = Cheese M = Mouse C = Cat		
1st 2nd 3rd	1st 2nd 3rd	1st 2nd 3rd
CH, C, M		
1st 2nd 3rd	1st 2nd 3rd	1st 2nd 3rd

To find the number without counting, do this:

<u>3 choices for 1st place</u> x <u>2 choices for 2nd place</u> x <u>1 choice for 3rd place</u>

3 x 2 x 1 = _____

Name the number of permutations for each of these:

1. five books on a shelf _____

2. four cars parked for the balloon race _____

3. three kids in line for tickets _____

4. eight wet suits hanging in a closet _____

5. six different skateboarding tricks _____

6. seven runners crossing the finish line _____

7. ten skiers waiting for a ski lift _____

8. four kayakers paddling down the river single file _____

Name _____

PARACHUTE COMBINATIONS

Before the jumpers head for the plane to start their day of skydiving practice, each one chooses two parachutes. On the outside, the parachute packages all look the same, but when the chutes open, the colors are different.

There are three parachutes laid out for each jumper: one red (R), one green (G), one yellow (Y). The jumper chooses two.

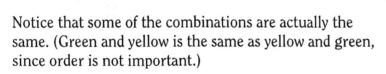

These are the combinations she might choose. (They are listed like this: 1st choice color, 2nd choice color.)

Notice that some of the combinations are actually the same. (Green and yellow is the same as yellow and green, since order is not important.)

Cross out the duplicate combinations.
How many possible combinations are there when choosing 2 out of 3 parachutes? _____

A. There are five prizes that can be won for a good jump: concert tickets (T), a giant pizza (P), a spaghetti dinner (D), movie tickets (M) or cash (C). The winner can choose 4 of the 5 prizes.

How many possible combinations are there of 4 prizes from 5? _____

Name them in the space below. Do not include duplicates.

B. The parachute club is forming pairs of jumpers from 6 jumpers: Ben (B), Carly (C), Daren (D), Evan (E), Fran (F), Georgia (G).

How many different pairs of jumpers can be formed from 6? _____

Name them in the space below. Do not include duplicates.

Name _____

NO LONGER JUST A SUMMER SPORT

What an idea! A snow-covered mountain may seem like the place for skiing or snowboarding. But some inventive folks thought of another use for steep snowy mountain trails . . . biking! Competitors race mountain bikes on snow in a new sport called Snow Mountain Biking.

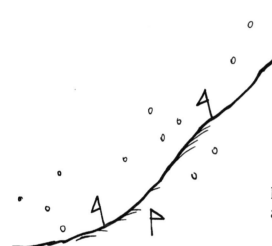

In this competition, each biker flips a coin to see which trail she or he will ride. Then, bikers roll a die to decide the order of the riders. When James rolls a die and flips a coin, there are several different possible outcomes of these two events.

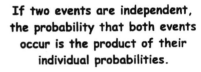

If two events are independent, the probability that both events occur is the product of their individual probabilities.

$$P(A \text{ and } B) = P(A) \times P(B)$$

OUTCOMES	
1 die roll & 1 coin toss	
H, 1	H, 2

Finish the table to show all the possible outcomes.

What is the probability of these?

Use the table to help you answer.

1. P(H and even number) =_____

2. P(T and even number) = _____

3. P(T and number > 2) = _____

4. P(H and 1, 2, 3, or 4) = _____

5. P(H and 4 or 5) =_____

6. P(T and number < 5) = _____

7. P(H and odd number) = _____

8. P(H and number > 1) =_____

9. P(T and multiple of 3) = _____

10. P(H and number > 4) =_____

11. P(T and number < 3) = _____

12. P(T and 1, 3, or 6) = _____

Name _____

WAITING FOR THE BIG ONE

Surfer Sal waits a long time for the best wave.

Of the next six waves, one will be 2 feet high, one will be 3 feet high, one will be 4 feet high, one will be 5 feet high, one will be 6 feet high, and one will be 7 feet high.

Sal will catch only one of them. When she does, she may ride it all the way, or she may wipe out!

What is the probability that she'll catch a 5-foot wave and ride it all the way?

$$P (5 \text{ and } R) = P (5) \times P (R) = \tfrac{1}{6} \times \tfrac{1}{2} = \tfrac{1}{12}$$

POSSIBLE OUTCOMES

Write all the possible outcomes for the events of catching the 2, 3, 4, 5, 6, or 7-foot wave and falling (F) or riding (R) the wave.

Find these probabilities:

1. Probability of catching a wave over 3 feet and falling.

    $P(4, 5, \text{ or } 6 \text{ and } F) = P (3) \times P (F) = $ _____ $\times$ _____ $=$ _____

2. Probability of catching a wave under 4 feet and riding it.

    $P(2 \text{ or } 3 \text{ and } R) = $ _____

Finish the table. Fill in an answer for each ?

	EVENTS	P(1st Event)	P (2nd Event)	(Both Events)
3) Toss a coin twice	H, H	$P(H) = \tfrac{1}{2}$	$P(H) = \tfrac{1}{2}$	$P(H \text{ and } H) = ?$
4) Roll a die, toss a coin	4, T	$P(4) = ?$	$P(T) = ?$	$P(4 \text{ and } T) = ?$
5) Toss a coin, Roll a die	T, even #	$P(T) = ?$	$P(\text{even \#}) = ?$	$P(6 \text{ and even \#}) = ?$
6) Roll a die, Toll a die	4, 4	$P(4) = ?$	$P(4) = ?$	$P(4 \text{ and } 4) = ?$

Name

UNBELIEVABLE BALLOON FLIGHTS

People actually take flights with toy balloons. Of course, they use dozens of large, sturdy balloons. The record-holder for this sport used 400 helium-filled toy balloons to fly to a height of 1 mile, 1575 yards.

This bunch of balloons has 200 red, 20 blue, 10 green, and 70 orange.

Suppose two pop. The probability of the 1st being green is $^{10}/_{300}$. What is the probability that the 2nd popping balloon is blue? The results are affected by the fact that one of the original balloons is gone. The probability of this second event is $^{20}/_{299}$.

The probability that both these events will happen is shown like this:

P(G and B) = P(G green) x (B/G blue given that green popped first)

P(G and B) = $^{10}/_{300}$ x $^{20}/_{299}$ = $^{200}/_{89,700}$ or $^{2}/_{897}$

Two balloons pop in each of the events below.

Finish the table to find the probabilities.

Original Balloon Bunch	1st Event (1st Popping Balloon)	2nd Event (2nd Popping Balloon)	Probability of Both Events
1) 2 red 1 green 4 blue 3 orange 2 yellow	P (Y) = ?	P (O) = ?	P (Y and O) = ?
2) 10 red 20 yellow 10 blue	P (B) = ?	P (R) = ?	P (B and R) = ?
3) 3 red 4 green 8 blue 5 yellow	P (Y) = ?	P (Y) = ?	P (Y and Y) = ?
4) 2 red 2 green 2 blue 2 orange 2 yellow 2 purple	P (G) = ?	P (G) = ?	P (G and G) = ?
5) 96 red 4 purple	P(P) = ?	P (R) = ?	P (P and R) = ?

Name

THOSE WACKY, WILD, WING-WALKERS

Here's another daredevil sport . . . walking on the wings of flying airplanes. Yes, people actually have done this for sport! Don't try it on your next airplane trip though.

These wing-walkers have a chance of winning prizes.

When they land successfully, each can draw an envelope from a group of five. Three of the envelopes have prizes, and two do not.

The **odds in favor** of getting a prize are 3 to 2.

The **odds against** getting a prize are 2 to 3.

Odds are different from probability.
But if you know the odds, you can find the probability.

Find the odds and probabilities for the prize possibilities below.

1. **7 boxes; 3 contain a prize**

   a. odds in favor of getting a prize = _____

   b. odds against getting a prize = _____

   c. probability of getting a prize = _____

2. **4 boxes; 1 contains a prize**

   a. odds in favor of a prize = _____

   b. odds against a prize = _____

   c. probability of NO prize = _____

3. **8 envelopes; 5 contain cash**

   a. odds in favor of getting cash = _____

   b. odds against getting cash = _____

   c. probability of getting cash = _____

4. **6 boxes; 2 contain prizes**

   a. odds in favor of a prize = _____

   b. odds against a prize = _____

   c. probability of NO prize = _____

5. **10 envelopes; 7 contain prizes**

   a. odds in favor of a prize = _____

   b. odds against a prize = _____

   c. probability of NO prize = _____

6. **9 boxes; 8 contain a prize**

   a. probability of getting a prize = _____

   b. odds in favor of getting a prize = _____

   c. odds against getting a prize = _____

7. **11 envelopes; 1 contains cash**

   a. odds in favor of getting cash = _____

   b. odds against getting cash = _____

   c. probability of getting cash = _____

8. **12 envelopes; 9 contain cash**

   a. probability of NOT getting cash = _____

   b. odds in favor of getting cash = _____

   c. odds against getting cash = _____

Name _____

SOCK PROBLEMS

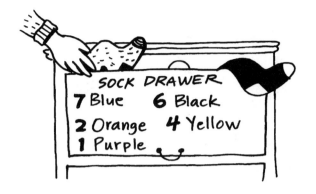

SOCK DRAWER
7 Blue   **6** Black
2 Orange   **4** Yellow
1 Purple

She's late for the downhill race, and Sasha can't find the right socks. She's reaching in this drawer and madly pulling out socks. The drawer is labeled with the numbers and colors of the socks.

Refer to Sasha's sock drawer to solve the probability problems below.

If Sasha pulls out one sock . . .

1. What is P (black)? .... _____
2. What is P (not yellow)? .... _____
3. What are the odds in favor of getting purple?............. _____
4. What are the odds in favor of getting blue? .... _____
5. What are the odds against getting black? .... _____

If Sasha gets a blue sock on her first grab . . .

6. What is P(blue) on her second try? .... _____
7. What is P (orange) on her second try? .... _____

If Sasha pulls out 2 socks at once . . .

8. What is P (yellow and black)? .... _____
9. What is P (orange and blue)?...................................... _____
10. What is P (purple and blue)? .... _____
11. What is P (2 blue socks)? .... _____
12. What is P (2 orange socks)?...................................... _____

13. You approach 20 skiers on the way to the race.
    8 are males, 12 are females.
    6 are wearing black gloves. 14 are wearing red gloves.
    You pass the first skier. What is the probability that this skier is . . .
    a. P (male wearing red gloves) =................................ _____
    b. P (female wearing red gloves) =............................ _____
    c. P (female wearing no gloves) =............................. _____
    d. P (male wearing black gloves) =........................... _____

Name

EXTREME JUGGLING

Jacko can juggle lots of stuff at the same time.
Balls are the ordinary things to juggle, but he also is
great with plates, vegetables, kitchen supplies, and shoes.

He has a huge bag with 1200 items of three kinds: shoes, tomatoes, and teacups. To estimate the probability of choosing any
one item when he reaches in the bag to grab something, some
friends sampled the items. Each of six friends chose 4 items
from the bag (in each case, taking the first thing they
touched) then replaced them. The table shows
the results of their samples.

Use the table to estimate the
probability for each kind of
item in the sample.

1. P (shoes) = _____

2. P (tomatoes) = _____

3. P (teacups) = _____

4. P (shoes or teacups) = _____

5. P (not shoes) = _____

6. P (not tomatoes) = _____

Out of 1200 items, predict
the number that would be:

7. shoes _____

8. tomatoes _____

9. teacups _____

10. A sampling of 30 athletes at
the Extreme Competition
found 6 with measles.

Predict the number out of all
900 athletes that had measles.

_____

11. A bag of Ener-G Bars contains
2400 bars. A random
sampling of 40 showed
these results:
12 chocolate, 15 caramel,
5 banana, 8 marshmallow.

Predict the number of
each bar in the bag:

a. chocolate = _____

b. caramel = _____

c. banana = _____

d. marshmallow = _____

Results of Sampling of Items for Juggling			
Friend	Shoes (S)	Tomatoes (T)	Cups (C)
Jimbo	2	0	2
Angie	1	1	2
Marco	0	1	3
Sal	1	0	3
Bobbo	2	1	1
Franco	0	1	3
Totals			

Name

APPENDIX

CONTENTS

TERMS FOR GRAPHING, STATISTICS, & PROBABILITY

Average — Synonym for mean: the sum of all the items in a given set of data divided by the number of items

Bar Graph — a graph that represents data with bars

Circle Graph — a graph that represents data by showing a circle divided into segments

Combination — a selection of a set of things from a larger set without regard to order

Counting Principle — a way to find the number of possible outcomes of an event with multiple stages: the total number of possible outcomes is the product of the outcomes of each stage

Data — information that is given in numerical form

Dependent Events — two events in which the result of the first event affects the outcome of the second event

Double Bar Graph — a graph that uses bars to compare two sets of data at the same time

Double Line Graph — a graph that uses two lines to compare the change in two sets of data over time

Event — a set of one or more outcomes

Frequency — the number of times an item appears in a set of data

Frequency Graph — a pictorial or graphic representation of frequencies of data

Frequency Polygram — a geometric curve shape formed when the dots are placed at the top center of each bar on a bar graph, then connected with a line

Frequency Table — a chart or table which summarizes and presents frequency data

Histogram — a bar graph showing frequency data

Independent Events — events whose outcomes have no effect on later events

Interval — amount of space or time

Line Graph — a graph that uses lines to show changes in data over time

Mean — the sum of data items divided by the number of items

Basic Skills/Graphing, Statistics, & Probability 6-8+　　Copyright ©2000 by Incentive Publications, Inc., Nashville, TN.

Counting Principle Total — a way to find the number of possible outcomes of an event with multiple stages: the total number of possible outcomes is the product of the outcomes of each stage

Median — the number that falls in the middle of a set of data when all the data items are arranged in order

Mode — the number or numbers in a set of data which appear most frequently

Multiple Line Graph — a line graph that shows more than one set of data changes on a single graph

Odds — the numerical likelihood of a chosen outcome in comparison to another

Odds Against — the numerical chance that an outcome will not be chosen

Odds in Favor — the numerical chance that an outcome will be chosen

Outcome — the result of a probability experiment

Permutation — an arrangement of data in a definite order

Pictograph — a graph which uses symbols or pictures to represent numerical data

Prediction — the projection into the future of possible outcomes, based on data at hand

Probability — a number describing the chance that an event will happen

Random — a description of an event that is a matter of chance, where different outcomes are equally likely to occur

Range — the difference between the greatest number and the least number in a collection of data

Ratio — the comparison of two numbers or quantities to each other in a fraction form

Relative Frequency — the ratio of the frequency of an item to the total frequencies

Sampling — a method of gaining data from a selection of a larger amount of data, in order to make predictions about larger amounts

Scattergram — a graph that shows the relationship between two quantities

Statistics — the collection, organization, interpretation, use, and/or study of numerical information

Survey — a way to collect numerical information by gathering data from several people or sources

Tree Diagram — a pictorial way to show possible outcomes of an activity

GRAPHING, STATISTICS, & PROBABILITY
SKILLS TEST

Each correct answer is worth 1 point. Total possible score: 100.

Choose the matching term for each definition. Write the letter on the line.

a. histogram   d. statistics   h. mean
b. data   e. frequency   i. scattergram
c. median   f. mode   j. range
                 g. line graph

_____ 1. the number of times an item appears in a set of data

_____ 2. information given in numerical form

_____ 3. a bar graph showing frequency data

_____ 4. the average of a number of data items

_____ 5. the collection, organization, and interpretation of sets of numerical data

_____ 6. the number that appears most often in a set of data

_____ 7. the difference between the least and greatest numbers in a set of data

_____ 8. a graph that shows the relationship between two items

_____ 9. a graph that uses lines to show changes in data over time

_____ 10. the number that falls in the middle of a set of data arranged in order

Use this frequency table for questions 11–14.

Number of Extreme Sports Events Held in Crash County, 1994-2000				
Sport	1994	1996	1998	2000
Wakeboarding	14	18	21	26
Barefoot Skiing	3	5	5	12
Jet Skiing	39	28	24	30
Windsurfing	0	1	4	6
Skysurfing	0	0	4	9
Dirt Bike Jumping	20	18	19	20

11. Which kind of sporting event was held most frequently over the years shown?

_____

12. How many sports increased in events from 1994 to 2000? _____

13. Which sport nearly doubled in number of events?

_____

14. Which quadrupled in number of events?

_____

Use this graph to answer questions 15–20.

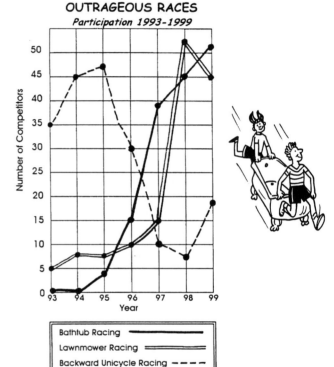

OUTRAGEOUS RACES
Participation 1993-1999

Bathtub Racing ————
Lawnmower Racing ═════
Backward Unicycle Racing – – – –

15. Which races had less than 35 competitors in 1996?

_____

_____

16. Which sport made the greatest gain in competitors from 1995 to 1999?

_____

17. Which sport had the greatest loss in participation? _____

18. Did the lawnmower races have more total participants in '95–'97 than the backward unicycle races? _____

19. In which year were the 3 sports closest in number of competitors? _____

20. Which sport made the greatest gain in participation between '98 and '99?

_____

Name _____

Use this Data Table for questions 21–29.

MOTORCYCLE JUMPS					
Numbers of Cars Jumped During Contest					
BIKER	Mon	Tue	Wed	Thur	Fri
J. J.	12	14	5	9	0
R. J.	16	15	15	15	14
P. J.	7	9	10	10	7
L. J.	12	10	8	7	15
T. J.	15	8	6	15	0

21. What is the mean of J. J.'s jumps? _____
22. What is the mode of all the data on the table? _____
23. What is the mean of R. J.'s jumps? _____
24. Who has the greatest range in jumps? _____
25. What is the median for Wednesday? _____
26. What is the mean for Friday's jumps? _____
27. What is the median of L. J.'s jumps? _____
28. What is the range of the data on the table? _____
29. What is the mean of T. J.'s jumps? _____

Use this graph for questions 30–34.

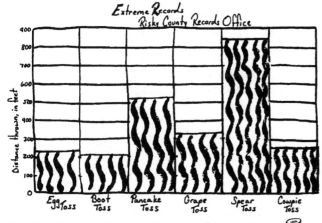

30. Which record was a distance about twice the egg toss? _____
31. Which toss was about 200 less than the pancake toss? _____
32. Which records were the closest? _____
_____
33. Which record was about 500 less than the spear toss? _____
34. Which record was about 600 more than the cowpie toss? _____

Use this Data Table for questions 35–39.

TICKETS SOLD ON ROLLERCOASTERS			
Rollercoaster	June	July	August
Tsunami	20,110	14,980	6,050
The Tarantula	5,070	9,310	6,800
The Terminator	12,400	24,100	17,700
Toronto Twister	10,000	10,900	10, 500
Tummy Turner	3,100	8,650	9,700
Texas Torture	8,020	5,070	16,300

35. Which coaster dropped in ticket sales between June and July? _____
36. Which coaster made the biggest gain in ticket sales between June and August? _____
37. Which coaster made the biggest gain in ticket sales between June and July? _____
38. Overall, which month was the best for ticket sales on the coasters? _____
39. Which coaster sold almost 5 times as many tickets in July as The Tarantula sold in June? _____

Use this graph for questions 40–44.

Injuries at Winter Competitions
January 20-30

Snow Mobile Racing
Ice Climbing
Snow Mountain Biking
Freestyle Skiing
Snow- boarding

5 10 15 20 25 30 35 40 45 50

■ - # of competitors   ▩ - # of injuries

40. Which sport had more than one injury per athlete? _____
41. Which 2 sports had 15 less competitors than snowmobile racing? _____
_____
42. Which sport had the fewest number of injuries in relation to the number of competitors? _____
43. Which sport had an injury for just less than half of its competitors? _____
44. Did any sport have about one injury for every 3 competitors? _____

Name

Use this circle graph for questions 45–47.

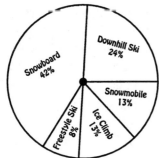

Competition Accidents

45. What % of the accidents were not ski accidents? _____

46. Which sports had a combined accident rate of 26%?
_____

47. What % of the accidents were skiing or snowboarding accidents? _____

Write the letter of the correct definition for each term.

____ 48. combination   ____ 52. random

____ 49. dependent events ____ 53. probability

____ 50. independent   ____ 54. permutation
events   ____ 55. outcomes

____ 51. sampling   ____ 56. event

  a. two events in which the result of the first affects the outcome of the second

  b. events that have equal probability of occurring

  c. a method of getting data from a selection from a larger amount of data, in order to make predictions about the larger amounts

  d. events whose outcomes have no effect on future events

  e. a number describing the chance that an event will happen

  f. the result of a probability experiment

  g. a selection of a set of things from a larger set without regard to order

  h. an arrangement of data in a particular order

  i. a set of one or more outcomes

Write the probability for each event. Use 0 or 1 or any fractional number in between.

_____ 57. 2 odd #s will have an even sum

_____ 58. a toss of a die will yield a 6

_____ 59. a flipped coin will land on tails

_____ 60. 2 odd numbers will have an odd sum

_____ 61. a month begins with the letter M

Write the number of possible outcomes for each of the following:

____ 62. Flip of a coin   ____ 65. Toss one die
____ 63. Toss of one die   and flip a coin.
____ 64. You'll be sick one   ____ 66. Flip a coin
day next week.   twice.

Use this spinner to answer questions 67–70.

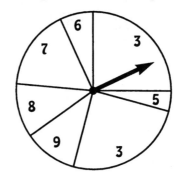

67. How many possible outcomes? _____

68. Which is most likely? _____

69. Which is least likely? _____

70. Which are equally likely? _____

71. Joe, a sky diver, is in a contest that he has a chance of winning or losing. At the end of the contest, ALL competitors will be given an envelope that has one of these amounts in it: $10, $20, $50, $100. There is an equal chance he could get any of the amounts of money.

  What are all the possible outcomes of the race and his winnings? Write the outcomes in the box. Use a letter and amount (such as W50 or L20, where W stands for win and L stands for lose).

┌─────────────────────────────────┐
│   │
│   │
└─────────────────────────────────┘

72. Toss a coin. P(H) = _____

73. Toss 2 coins. P(TT) = _____

74. Toss 2 coins. P(one H and one T) = _____

75. Toss 1 die. P(odd #) = _____

76. Toss 1 die P(# < 5) = _____

77. Toss 1 die, flip 1 coin P(H, #<6)= _____

78. Toss 1 die, flip 1 coin P(H, 4) = _____

79. Toss 1 die, flip 1 coin P(H, #<4) _____

80. Toss 1 die, flip 1 coin P(T, odd #) = _____

81. Toss 2 dice. P(6,5) = _____

82. Toss 2 dice. P(both # same) = _____

83. Toss 2 dice. P(sum of 6) = _____

Name

Charlene will race in two handsprinting races against 4 other sprinters. She could come in 1st through 5th in either race.

84. What is the number of possible outcomes for her two races? _____

85. What is the probability of 1st and 3rd place finishes? _____

86. What is the probability of no 1st place finishes? _____

87. What is the probability that she'll finish in the same place both days? _____

88. Before biking, Bob goes to his sock drawer. It contains 5 red, 7 white, 3 purple socks. He grabs one out without looking. It is red. What is the probability that the second one is purple? _____

89. Yesterday, his drawer had 5 red and 4 white socks. What is the probability he would draw a red on the first grab and a white on the second grab? _____

90. Tom reaches into a bag of 100 snorkels, and chooses one. The pulls out 5, then returns them and takes out 5 a few more times. After a sampling of 25 snorkels, he finds that 5 of the 25 were broken. Predict the number of snorkels that will probably be broken in the whole bag of 100.

_____

91. After a long dive, Tom and his friends take a random sample of 30 Ener-G bars from a bag of 3000. The sample yielded 5 cinnamon, 15 peach, 4 apple, and 6 fudge. Predict the number of each kind of bar in the bag of 3000:

_____ 91. cinnamon

_____ 92. apple

_____ 93. peach

_____ 94. fudge

95. Three envelopes. Two contain cash. Choose one envelope.

a. Odds in favor of getting cash _____

b. Odds against getting cash _____

c. Probability of getting cash _____

96. Seven envelopes. Five contain cash.
a. Probability of NOT getting cash _____
b. Odds in favor of getting cash _____
c. Odds against getting cash _____

These 3 skiers will end the race in 1st–3rd places. What are the possible arrangements of order (permutations) in which they might finish?

97. The number of arrangements _____

98. List the possible arrangements

_____

_____

99. How many permutations (possible different arrangements) are there of 5 ski outfits hanging in a closet? _____

100. Two of the skiers arrive at the finish line at exactly the same time. How many possibilities are there for the make-up of that pair? _____ List the possible combinations of two skiers who finish at the same time: _____

SCORE: Total Points _____ out of a possible 100 points

Name

GRAPHING, STATISTICS, & PROBABILITY
SKILLS TEST ANSWER KEY

Questions are worth 1 point each.

1. e
2. b
3. a
4. h
5. d
6. f
7. j
8. i
9. g
10. c
11. jet skiing
12. 4
13. wakeboarding
14. barefoot skiing
15. all 3 (bathtub races, backward unicycle races, lawnmower races)
16. bathtub races
17. backward unicycle races
18. yes
19. 1996
20. backwards unicycle races
21. 8
22. 15
23. 15
24. T. J.
25. 8
26. 7.2
27. 10
28. 0–16
29. 8.8
30. pancake toss
31. grape toss
32. egg toss, and boot toss
33. grape toss
34. spear toss
35. Texas Torture and Tsunami
36. Texas Torture
37. Terminator

38. July
39. The Terminator
40. snowboarding
41. ice climbing and snowboarding
42. snowmobile racing
43. freestyle skiing
44. no
45. 68%
46. snowmobile and ice climb
47. 74%
48. g
49. a
50. d
51. c
52. b
53. e
54. h
55. f
56. i
57. 1
58. $\frac{1}{6}$
59. $\frac{1}{2}$
60. 0
61. $\frac{2}{12}$ or $\frac{1}{6}$
62. 2
63. 6
64. 7
65. 12
66. 4
67. 6
68. 3
69. 5
70. 8, 9
71. W10, W20, W50, W100, L10, L20, L50, L100
72. $\frac{1}{2}$

73. $\frac{1}{4}$
74. $\frac{2}{4}$ or $\frac{1}{2}$
75. $\frac{3}{6}$ or $\frac{1}{2}$
76. $\frac{4}{6}$ or $\frac{2}{3}$
77. $\frac{5}{12}$
78. $\frac{1}{12}$
79. $\frac{3}{12}$ or $\frac{1}{4}$
80. $\frac{3}{12}$ or $\frac{1}{4}$
81. $\frac{6}{36}$
82. $\frac{6}{36}$ or $\frac{1}{6}$
83. $\frac{5}{36}$
84. 25
85. $\frac{2}{25}$
86. $\frac{16}{25}$
87. $\frac{5}{25}$ or $\frac{1}{5}$
88. $\frac{3}{42}$ or $\frac{1}{14}$
89. $\frac{5}{18}$
90. 20
91. 500
92. 400
93. 1500
94. 600
95. a. $\frac{2}{1}$
    b. $\frac{1}{2}$
    c. $\frac{2}{3}$
96. a. $\frac{2}{7}$
    b. $\frac{5}{2}$
    c. $\frac{2}{5}$
97. 6
98. ABC, ACB, BCA, BAC, CAB, CBA
99. 120
100. 3; A & B, A & C, B & C

ANSWERS

page 10

Frequency Table Data:

JTSK-7	STLG-1
WSRF-4	HGGD-4
AILS-6	SKYS-4
BFJP-2	WKBD-5
BCYS-2	SPCL-4
SKBD-5	BNGY-7

page 11

Frequency Table Data:

AK-9	ID-6	NM-2
AL-2	LA-1	NY-1
AR-1	ME-4	OR-8
AZ-1	MI-2	SC-2
CA-17	MN-1	TX-3
CO-15	MO-1	WA-9
FL-5	MT-8	UT-4
GA-1	NC-1	VT-3
HI-20	NJ-1	

page 12

Some answers may be approximate. Give student credit if the answer is close for #8 and #9.

1. 40-45
2. 60-65
3. 35-40
4. 30-35
5. 20-25
6. 10-15
7. 50
8. about 12
9. about 75
10. 35-40 or 10-15
11. 60-65, 65-70, over 70
12. 45-50 and 55-60
13. 40-50
14. 35-40
15. 35-40
16. yes

page 13

Check graph to see that the heights of bars match these tallies from the tally sheet:

```
        0-500 mi . . . 58
    500-1000 mi . . . 73
  1000-1500 mi . . . 55
  1500-2000 mi . . . 61
  2000-2500 mi . . . 38
     over 2500 mi . . . 20
```

page 14

1. spear
2. grape
3. spear
4. 13 ft, 5 in
5. 638 ft, 9½ in
6. 19 ft
7. 846 mi, 1375 yd
8. spear
9. motorcycle jump
10. 34,872 ft

page 15

1. 47
2. 74
3. 11
4. 64
5. 27
6. 23
7. 48
8. 65
9. 13
10. 15
11. 25
12. 12
13. 95
14. 89
15. 62
16. Rapids Racers
17. River Racers
18. White Water Wizards
19. Unsinkables
20. Tuesday
21. Friday
22. White Water Wizards

page 16

1. 3–21
2. 11
3. 2-7; 4
4. 90 lb–140 lb; 109
5. 0–16; 8¼
6. 15–32; 19

page 17

Complete the chart with these totals.
Median, across . . . 15, 15, 15, 12, 14
Mode, across . . . 11, 27, 21, 20, 9

1. 15
2. 36
3. 12
4. circle 101 lb,
   squares around 77 lb and 77 lb

page 18

1. August
2. 460 m
3. September
4. 220 m
5. February
6. 450 m
7. April
8. October and May
9. 60 m

page 19

Answers for 1, 2, 9 may not be exactly as given below. Give credit if the number is close.

1. 3600
2. 6200
3. Sly
4. 4
5. Sue
6. Shirl
7. 5000
8. Sam
9. 3500
10. Shirl
11. Sara
12. Sam or Sly

page 20

Check student graph to see that the data from the table has been accurately plotted and line has been drawn in order from dive 1–12.

page 21

Check student graph to see that the data from the table has been accurately transferred to the graph.

page 22

Check student graph to see that the data from the table has been accurately transferred to the graph.

page 23

1. 6
2. 10
3. 6
4. 11
5. 5 ft
6. 1 ft
7. 7 ft
8. no
9. no
10. yes
11. 4
12. 11 and 12 ft
13. 8
14. 14
15. a, d, f

page 24

1. Nicole
2. Jennifer
3. Brandy
4. Nicole
5. Amanda
6. Jennifer
7. yes
8. above
9. 8 and 9
10. 5 and 6
11. Jennifer
12. Nicole

page 25

Check student graph to see that the data from the table has been accurately plotted and that each line has been drawn in proper color and in correct sequential order of the years.

page 26

1. 5½ or 6 min
2. Midnight Kings
3. Sleepwalkers
4. 11
5. 1 min
6. 3 min or 3½ min or 4 min
7. 1 min
8. 32
9. Snooze Crew and Sleepwalkers
10. Answers may vary. The teams with more experience have faster times.

page 27

Check student graph to see that the data from the table has been accurately transferred to the graph. Make sure alternate bars are green and yellow as instructed.

page 28

1. 230200 mi
2. bicycle

3. 4900 mi
4. 847 mi
5. Answers will vary
6. Answers will vary
7. Answers will vary
8. Answers will vary
9. 2308 mi
10. Answers will vary

page 29

1. 6
2. 13
3. 4
4. 19
5. 27
6. 7
7. yes
8. 22
9. half cab
10. slob heli
11. yes
12. no

page 30

1. 45 years (answer is approximate)
2. 40
3. Bob, Boe, Brad
4. no
5. 25
6. 11 (answer is approximate)
7. x = Brett; y = Bev
8. x = Benjy; y = Brad
9. a = Brad; b = Bob
10. 30

page 31

1. 678 ft
2. 27 ft
3. Flo or Frank or Fred
4. Phoebe
5. Phillipe
6. Frank
7. Phyllis
8. 0
9. 195 ft
10. Phyllis
11. 6
12. 91 ft
13. 920 ft
14. 10

pages 32–33

1. 139 hours
2. MA
3. 39 hours
4. 113 hours
5. 103 hours
6. 1055 hours
7. CA
8. Black Widow
9. Swamp Fox
10. 16 hours
11. 67 hours
12. Maria; 2 hours
13. Big Bad Wolf
14. Brianna

15. Texas Twister, Tidal Wave, Twisted Sisters; 156 hours
16. Outlaw

page 34–35

Answers may vary slightly. Give credit for answers that approximate these:

1. 1.84
2. 10 ft
3. 1872
4. no
5. no
6. 0.1202 sec or .1202 sec
7. 208
8. 0.04 sec or .04 sec
9. 0.73 sec or .73 sec
10. 2.13 sec
11. 1620
12. yes
13. 300
14. no
15. 780
16. 2 min, 32.9 sec
17. $7\frac{1}{2}$ min
18. 3 min

page 36

1. 152
2. P. J.
3. 17.25
4. yes
5. R. J. and J. J.
6. 13
7. J. J.
8. R. J.s
9. P. J.
10. B. J. and R. J.
11. B. J.
12. R. J.
13. J. J.s
14. 17

page 37

1. $\frac{1}{4}$
2. $\frac{1}{4}$
3. $\frac{2}{4}$ or $\frac{1}{2}$
4. $\frac{2}{4}$ or $\frac{1}{2}$
5. 1
6. $\frac{1}{2}$
7. 1
8. 0
9. 0
10. $\frac{1}{6}$
11. 1
12. Answers will vary
13. $\frac{1}{50}$
14. 1
15. 2
16. 6
17. $\frac{3}{12}$ or $\frac{1}{4}$
18. $\frac{2}{7}$
19. 5
20. E
21. C
22. A and B

page 38

1. $\frac{1}{6}$
2. $\frac{2}{6}$ or $\frac{1}{3}$
3. $\frac{1}{6}$
4. $\frac{3}{6}$ or $\frac{1}{2}$
5. $\frac{4}{6}$ or $\frac{2}{3}$
6. $\frac{2}{6}$ or $\frac{1}{3}$
7. $\frac{1}{6}$
8. $\frac{3}{6}$ or $\frac{1}{2}$
9. $\frac{3}{6}$ or $\frac{1}{2}$
10. $\frac{2}{6}$ or $\frac{1}{3}$
11. $\frac{2}{6}$ or $\frac{1}{3}$
12. $\frac{4}{6}$ or $\frac{2}{3}$
13. $\frac{2}{6}$ or $\frac{1}{3}$
14. $\frac{3}{6}$ or $\frac{1}{2}$
15. $\frac{2}{6}$ or $\frac{1}{3}$
16. $\frac{5}{6}$
17. $\frac{1}{6}$
18. $\frac{2}{6}$ or $\frac{1}{3}$

page 39

Finish the graph

Totals across bottom: AR = 50, AC = 80,

M = 70, Total Tricks = 200
Totals down right: Japan = 50, Canada = 90, USA = 60, Total Skiers = 200

1. $\frac{90}{200}$ or $\frac{45}{100}$ or $\frac{9}{20}$
2. $\frac{140}{200}$ or $\frac{7}{10}$
3. $\frac{50}{200}$ or $\frac{1}{4}$
4. $\frac{30}{200}$ or $\frac{3}{20}$
5. $\frac{20}{200}$ or $\frac{1}{10}$
6. $\frac{120}{200}$ or $\frac{3}{5}$
7. $\frac{150}{200}$ or $\frac{3}{4}$
8. $\frac{130}{200}$ or $\frac{13}{20}$
9. $\frac{20}{200}$ or $\frac{1}{10}$
10. $\frac{50}{200}$ or $\frac{1}{4}$
11. $\frac{20}{60}$ or $\frac{1}{3}$
12. $\frac{40}{50}$ or $\frac{4}{5}$
13. $\frac{60}{90}$ or $\frac{2}{3}$
14. $\frac{10}{80}$ or $\frac{1}{8}$
15. $\frac{40}{50}$ or $\frac{4}{5}$
16. $\frac{40}{60}$ or $\frac{4}{6}$ or $\frac{2}{3}$
17. $\frac{30}{70}$ or $\frac{3}{7}$
18. $\frac{30}{50}$ or $\frac{3}{5}$
19. $\frac{50}{80}$ or $\frac{5}{8}$
20. $\frac{10}{50}$ or $\frac{1}{5}$

page 40

Outcomes for 2 spins . . . not necessarily in this order:
DD, DR, DN, RR, RD, RN, NN, ND, NR

Outcomes for 4 flips, not necessarily in this order:
HHHH, HHHT, HHTT, HTTT, HTHH, HTTH, HHTH, HTHT
TTTT, TTTH, TTHH, THHH, THHT, THTH, TTHT, THTT

1. $\frac{5}{9}$
2. $\frac{4}{9}$
3. $\frac{1}{9}$
4. $\frac{2}{9}$
5. $\frac{3}{9}$ or $\frac{1}{3}$
6. $\frac{6}{9}$ or $\frac{2}{3}$
7. $\frac{8}{16}$ or $\frac{1}{2}$
8. $\frac{6}{16}$ or $\frac{3}{8}$
9. $\frac{4}{16}$ or $\frac{1}{4}$
10. $\frac{2}{16}$ or $\frac{1}{8}$
11. $\frac{1}{16}$
12. $\frac{2}{16}$ or $\frac{1}{8}$

page 41

Outcomes for Rolling 2 dice, not necessarily in this orders;
1. 1.1, 1.2, 1.3, 1.4, 1.5, 1.6
2. 2.1, 2.2, 2.3, 2.4, 2.5, 2.6
3. 3.1, 3.2, 3.3, 3.4, 3.5, 3.6
4. 4.1, 4.2, 4.3, 4.4, 4.5, 4.6
5. 5.1, 5.2, 5.3, 5.4, 5.5, 5.6
6. 6.1, 6.2, 6.3, 6.4, 6.5, 6.6

1. $\frac{1}{36}$
2. $\frac{6}{36}$ or $\frac{1}{6}$
3. $\frac{9}{36}$ or $\frac{1}{4}$
4. $\frac{16}{36}$ or $\frac{4}{9}$
5. $\frac{9}{36}$ or $\frac{1}{4}$
6. $\frac{5}{36}$
7. $\frac{3}{36}$ or $\frac{1}{12}$
8. $\frac{5}{36}$

9. $^{18}/_{36}$ or $^{1}/_{2}$
10. $^{3}/_{36}$ or $^{1}/_{12}$
11. $^{6}/_{36}$ or $^{1}/_{6}$
12. $^{4}/_{36}$ or $^{1}/_{9}$
13. $^{4}/_{36}$ or $^{1}/_{9}$
14. $^{10}/_{36}$ or $^{5}/_{18}$
15. $^{2}/_{36}$ or $^{1}/_{18}$
16. $^{2}/_{36}$ or $^{1}/_{18}$

page 42

Outcomes:
GG, GO, GP, OG, OO, OP, PG, PO, PP
1. 9
2. $^{1}/_{9}$
3. $^{8}/_{9}$
4. $^{1}/_{9}$
5. $^{2}/_{9}$
6. $^{2}/_{9}$

page 43

Outcomes:
  1, 1; 1, 2; 1, 3; 1, 4; 1, 5;
  2, 1; 2, 2; 2, 3; 2, 4; 2, 5;
  3, 1; 3, 2; 3, 3; 3, 4; 3, 5;
  4, 1; 4, 2; 4, 3; 4, 4; 4, 5;
  5, 1; 5, 2; 5, 3; 5, 4; 5, 5
1. $^{3}/_{25}$ (2, 5; 5, 2; or 4, 4)
2. $^{1}/_{25}$ (1, 1)
3. $^{1}/_{25}$ (5, 5)
4. $^{2}/_{25}$ (2, 3 or 3, 2)
5. $^{2}/_{25}$ (5, 4 or 4, 5)
6. $^{2}/_{25}$ (3, 4 or 4, 3)
7. $^{2}/_{25}$ (3, 5 or 5, 3)
8. 0
9. $^{20}/_{25}$ (every outcome except 3, 5 or 5, 3; or 4, 4 or 5, 5)
10. $^{1}/_{25}$ (5, 5)
11. $^{3}/_{25}$ (2, 2 or 1, 5 or 5, 1)
12. 0

page 44

1. 2
2. 3
3. 3
4. 2 x 3 x 3 = 18
5. $^{1}/_{18}$
6. 36
7. 72
8. 48

page 45

Chart: Balloon Permutations . . . not necessarily in this order on chart:
CH, C, M
CH, M, C
C, CH, M
C, M, CH
M, CH, C
M, C, CH

Example: 6; 6
1. 120
2. 24
3. 6
4. 40,320
5. 720
6. 5040
7. 3,628,800
8. 24

page 46

Example: 3
A. 5 Combinations do not have to be listed in this exact order:
TPDM, TDMC, TPDC, TPMC, PDMC
B. 15 Combinations do not have to be listed in this exact order:
BC, BD, BE, BF, BG,
CD, CE, CF, CG,
DE, DF, DG,
EF, EG, FG

page 47

Outcomes not necessarily listed in this order: H1, H2, H3, H4, H5, H6,
T1, T2, T3, T4, T5, T6
1. $^{3}/_{12}$ or $^{1}/_{4}$
2. $^{3}/_{12}$ or $^{1}/_{4}$
3. $^{1}/_{12}$
4. $^{4}/_{12}$ or $^{1}/_{3}$
5. $^{2}/_{12}$ or $^{1}/_{6}$
6. $^{4}/_{12}$ or $^{1}/_{3}$
7. $^{3}/_{12}$ or $^{1}/_{4}$
8. $^{5}/_{12}$
9. $^{2}/_{12}$ or $^{1}/_{6}$
10. $^{2}/_{12}$ or $^{1}/_{6}$
11. $^{2}/_{12}$ or $^{1}/_{6}$
12. $^{3}/_{12}$ or $^{1}/_{4}$

page 48

Outcomes not necessarily listed in this order: 2R, 2F,
3R, 3F,
4R, 4F,
5R, 5F,
6R, 6F,
7R, 7F

1. $^{3}/_{6}$ x 1/2 = $^{3}/_{12}$ or $^{1}/_{4}$
2. $^{2}/_{6}$ x 1/2 = $^{2}/_{12}$ or $^{1}/_{6}$

Table:
Answers across:
3. $^{1}/_{2}$; $^{1}/_{2}$; $^{1}/_{4}$
4. $^{1}/_{6}$; $^{1}/_{2}$; $^{1}/_{12}$
5. $^{1}/_{2}$; $^{3}/_{6}$ or $^{1}/_{2}$; $^{1}/_{4}$ or $^{3}/_{12}$
6. $^{1}/_{6}$; $^{1}/_{6}$; $^{1}/_{36}$

page 49

Table, across
1. $^{2}/_{12}$ or $^{1}/_{6}$; $^{3}/_{11}$; $^{1}/_{22}$
2. $^{10}/_{40}$ or $^{1}/_{4}$; $^{10}/_{39}$; $^{5}/_{78}$
3. $^{5}/_{20}$ or $^{1}/_{4}$; $^{5}/_{19}$; $^{5}/_{76}$
4. $^{2}/_{12}$ or $^{1}/_{6}$; $^{2}/_{11}$; $^{1}/_{33}$
5. $^{4}/_{100}$ or $^{1}/_{25}$; $^{32}/_{33}$; $^{32}/_{825}$

page 50

1. a. $^{3}/_{4}$
  b. $^{4}/_{3}$
  c. $^{3}/_{7}$
2. a. $^{1}/_{3}$
  b. $^{3}/_{1}$
  c. $^{3}/_{4}$
3. a. $^{5}/_{3}$
  b. $^{3}/_{5}$
  c. $^{5}/_{8}$
4. a. $^{2}/_{4}$ or $^{1}/_{2}$
  b. $^{4}/_{2}$
  c. $^{4}/_{6}$ or $^{2}/_{3}$
5. a. $^{7}/_{3}$
  b. $^{3}/_{7}$
  c. $^{3}/_{10}$
6. a. $^{8}/_{9}$
  b. $^{8}/_{1}$
  c. $^{1}/_{8}$
7. a. $^{1}/_{10}$
  b. $^{10}/_{1}$
  c. $^{1}/_{11}$
8. a. $^{3}/_{12}$ or $^{1}/_{4}$
  b. $^{9}/_{3}$ or $^{3}/_{1}$
  c. $^{3}/_{9}$ or $^{1}/_{3}$

page 51

1. $^{6}/_{20}$ or $^{3}/_{10}$
2. $^{16}/_{20}$ or $^{4}/_{5}$
3. $^{1}/_{19}$
4. $^{7}/_{13}$
5. $^{14}/_{6}$ or $^{7}/_{3}$
6. $^{6}/_{19}$
7. $^{2}/_{19}$
8. $^{3}/_{50}$
9. $^{7}/_{200}$
10. $^{7}/_{400}$
11. $^{49}/_{400}$
12. $^{4}/_{400}$ or $^{1}/_{100}$
13. a. $^{112}/_{400}$ or $^{7}/_{25}$
  b. $^{168}/_{400}$ or $^{21}/_{50}$
  c. 0
  d. $^{48}/_{400}$ or $^{12}/_{100}$ or $^{3}/_{25}$

page 52

Chart:
Totals across: 6, 4, 14
1. $^{6}/_{24}$ or $^{1}/_{4}$
2. $^{4}/_{24}$ or $^{1}/_{6}$
3. $^{14}/_{24}$ or $^{7}/_{12}$
4. $^{20}/_{24}$ or $^{5}/_{6}$
5. $^{18}/_{24}$ or $^{6}/_{8}$ or $^{3}/_{4}$
6. $^{20}/_{24}$ or $^{5}/_{6}$
7. 300
8. 200
9. 700
10. 180
11. a. 720
  b. 900
  c. 300
  d. 480